AF248811

Midlife ~ Mid-Century ~ Mid-South

Midlife ~ Mid-Century ~ Mid-South

*The events and happenings of a Southern girl who
spent many happy and interesting years working
with beautiful furniture and nice people,
as told to her children and friends!*

BY VIRGINIA FORD ZENKE

CHAPEL HILL
PRESS, INC.

ISBN 1-59715-005-3
Library of Congress Catalog Number 2005931959

Printed in the United States of America
08 07 06 05 04 10 9 8 7 6 5 4 3 2 1

DEDICATED TO

Virginia Hawthorne Zenke
Henry Christian Zenke III
and the late
Henry Christian Zenke II

Acknowledgements

William Walter Burch
Carolyn Baxley Davis
Dr. Eric Emerson, Ph.D.
Martha Long
Mr. and Mrs. John S. May Jr.
Deborah King Melina
Richetta W. Roach
Diana Spindler-Jones
Misty Thebeau

Beginning

It has been said (and I do not know the origin of this thought) that between birth date and death date, there is only a long dash, which tells nothing of what went on during a person's life. Please consider these truthful episodes as a digest of dashes through my life.

All shared with my husband, Henry Christian Zenke II—Hank
my daughter, Virginia Hawthorne Zenke—Ginia
my son, Henry Christian Zenke III—Chris

Why?

There is no plot, no message, no beginning, and no ending. It is mainly my desire to share these events with those who might be interested and to publish something about happy living in North Carolina.

I think of so many published stories about the south that follow the same plot, small town or big city, and they include the endless and everlasting race problems, inner city and class distinctions, and politics over and over again in the same pattern. I would just like the reading public to know that some things happen in North Carolina and the South, and to people in North Carolina and the South, that are a little lighthearted and fun.

As Told by Virginia Ford Zenke...

CHARLESTON—In 1928, we were driving into Charleston, that most holy of Southern cities. I was sitting between my mother and father and feeling safe and secure. Daddy had just returned from foreign duty and we were moving to that "city by the sea." My earliest memory of this arrival was seeing patches of blue sky as it filtered through the beautiful gray moss, dripping (that's what Spanish moss does—it does not hang, it drips) from branches of large trees. All of this formed an archway and canopy into Charleston and painted an indelible memory that I would carry with me throughout my life, for Charleston became a cocoon I was encased in forever. To know me was to know Charleston!

The wonder and charm of the place of my birth, in Virginia, would not reappear until quite later in my life.

We arrived in time to see the city flooded. There must have been a hurricane to bring forth enough water for the Ashley and Cooper Rivers to meet at "the neck" well above the city. And it was a sight to see!

I had not yet started school, so my mother was my only playmate, and as we saw the sites of that beautiful city together, I loved every minute of it. The early morning street cries of the vendors in the city were something to remember. Among those who came our way was a fisherman who sold fish from door-to-door. I always wondered if he had Portuguese ancestry.

Apparently, he and my father had made arrangements for an early morning rendezvous of fishing. I can only believe that the fisherman talked daddy into this arrangement, for I have no memories of my father seeking out this type of entertainment. We were all invited to go along. I was supposed to be excited, but how excited can a four-year-old get at four o'clock in the morning? I do recall, however, the delicious breakfast we had. Mother made for us sandwiches of scrambled eggs with bacon on buttered bread. Also, my memory includes the flashing yellow lights at the railroad crossing as we passed North Charleston. We were going to Goose Creek and Back River. Who knows what wonderful old plantation sites (abandoned even then) we might have passed in the early morning darkness!

Mother and I stayed in the car, or walked in the woods, while the men fished in rowboats out on the water. Such a vivid picture of the "fisherman in his boat" was etched in my mind, again framed with gray moss and complete silence. The catch was in and a boat was dragged up on shore and turned over to form a table. A gourmet meal of freshly caught, cleaned, and fried fish with grits and cornbread is one of the very strong memories of that four-year-old. Father seemed to enjoy the morning, but I have, however, no memory of his pursuing fishing as a pastime after that.

Fifty-five years later the mail arrived one day with the announcement of an occasion in South Carolina, accompanied by an invitation to lunch in the country at one of the oldest plantation houses in the state. It was appealing and I accepted, and within a few days of the event, I mentioned it to Henry.

"Do you really want to go? I think we have already been there!" he argued.

"But I think this would be a nice thing to do and I would just like to be with my own kind and kin once in awhile. I've already accepted, so please, let's go."

We go.

A happy weekend was topped off with lunch, out at the plantation, in a cabin by the river that was especially designed for such occasions. It was in February, Bloody Marys were served to thirty guests in front of a roaring fire. Of course, there were people there whom we knew and among them Lady Astor's niece, Nancy Lancaster, who had visited us at our home in Virginia several years before. When the time came to be seated, our gracious hostess told us all to find our place cards, and it *was* time to be seated. I looked up to see Henry across the room, pointing first to my place card and then to me. There was some other message in what he was trying to tell me, but I paid no attention. I worked my way over to my designated seat and found that I was being seated by, and on the right hand side of almost God the Father—his grace, the Duke of Wellington! I think this brush with live history was a rare moment in my life. He was over from England for some low country hunting and was dressed accordingly in tweeds and knickers.

Conversation went very well. Thank goodness for my love of history, and for my ability to talk with him about his daughter-in-law's family, as well as his Spanish properties and connections.

This was, however, not the only highlight of my visit. After lunch, we all went up to the "big house" for further socializing. There were beautiful objects to observe. There were gorgeous flowers from the gardens and hothouse. Handsome portraits and paintings adorned the walls, and in the dining room one painting quickly caught my eye, jarred my memory, and stilled my soul. I could only stand transfixed before a small oil, depicting a lone fisherman in a rowboat in still water on Back River. Was it the old gentleman who had taken us fishing over half a century ago? It had to be. For me it was!

———•◆•———

THE HARTFORD—While still a small child in Charleston, much time was spent visiting the sights of the old Navy Yard. We would shop at the commissary, get medicine from the sick bay, and call on the captain's wife, Mrs. Ancrum at Marshlands, the plantation house that was the sight of the navy yard, now moved.

Docked, at that time, was the old navy ship, Hartford, which was such a prominent part of the Battle of Mobile Bay, during the late unpleasantness. It was Admiral Farragut's flagship and now, in the 1930's, it had been towed, dismasted, to Charleston. Without its mast, it looked like Noah's ark as written and pictured in books and magazines, and to think I was allowed to play on it, run up and down its decks. Such a thrill, and I lived to see it towed to the Norfolk navy yard and left in the Elizabeth River marshes to disintegrate. I have a picture that I took of it in crumbling condition on the Berkley side of the river.

So much history, so callously handled and tossed about. It really had been a beautiful ship.

FRANCES MARION—One of the giants of history who has been a part of my life is Francis Marion. A partisan warrior who formed a band known as Marion's Men to help in the American Revolution, "the Swamp Fox."

When I was a child and we would travel from Charleston to my grandparents home in a county called Marion, we would have to go through the Frances Marion Swamp and cross the Santee River. My father often teased me when we talked about those historic events.

"Look, look, Virginia, over there behind that tree, there he is on his horse."

"Where? Daddy, where?

"Oh, you missed him, but he will be around."

And around he has always been. I actually saw a letter he had written. It was in a private home in South Carolina. I do not remember what the letter said, but I recall his small, even handwriting and the fact that he spelled the word quiet, "quiot."

As close as I had been to the spot, I had never been to his well-marked gravesite. We were having lunch with friends near Aiken (lunch in rural South Carolina is having a big dinner at two or three o'clock in the afternoon). We had an appointment to meet someone down at the coast near Georgetown at 7:00 P.M.

Now, it is easy to go anywhere from north to south on *good roads down south*, but going from west to east is a different matter.

I told Henry that if we could stick to the back roads, we might get there on time, and that's what we had to do anyway. Getting across all the creeks and rivers takes a bit of doing, and I do believe that in order to get anywhere in South Carolina you have to cross Lynches River several times. Anyway, I saw by the map that one devious route would take us through a spot called Eutawville. And guess what? Plotting time again. It would be terrible to be so close and not stop by the grave of my hero, Francis Marion, the "Swamp Fox."

After many miles of devious routes, Henry would say, "Why are we turning this way?"

"Oh, it looks like a short cut," replied Virginia.

Sure enough, finally there was the road sign marking the spot one half of a mile away: "Grave of Francis Marion, Revolutionary War Hero."

"Oh Hank, it would be a shame not to see it. We are so close. It will only take a minute."

Pause.

"Please?"

"Very well," Henry relented.

We were traveling in a Jaguar, a comfortable, lovely car. This was before Jaguars began to look like all other cars. Darkness and the sunset through the moss on the trees made it all very "spooky." As we turned into the little family cemetery, I could only gasp.

Let me qualify my gasps. My father always said that I would die of sunburned tonsils!

Suddenly, there was a life-sized white specter sitting on the fence, contemplating. It could only be the spirit of Francis Marion that I viewed. It was! It was! It was! With the gasp, Henry turned the lights of the car on and the apparition disappeared. Anyone who had whipped the British certainly was not going to linger in the presence of a British-made mode of transportation.

Many years later, enough research produced a list of Marion's men who had served with him and there it was: Captain James Ford, my father's great, great, great grandfather.

We finally arrived at the coast only thirty minutes late.

<hr />

Our work seems to demand that we tackle summer homes in the dead of winter, and winter homes in the heat of summer. This was the occasion when my son and I found ourselves on the waterfront of the Atlantic Ocean on that historic coast where LaFayette landed centuries ago, as seen from the coast of South Carolina in a high wind on a very cold day. It is a favorite spot of mine in any weather. The history of that area, Waccamaw Neck, has always fascinated me. And the wonderful stories of my hero, Francis Marion, better known as "The Swamp Fox," never fail to interest me. Standing in the middle of a new house-to-be with no walls up—my attention span was waning—in fact, maybe disappearing. The presence of clients, the architect, the contractor, engineers, and staff, as well as myself and the noise of a power saw, all made me blank out. I turned and went to the edge of the flooring and just stared and stared at the wonderful winter landscape of marshes. I soon felt comfort at the touch of my elbow. My son, who reads my thoughts and moods so well, was pointing into the marshes.

"Look Mom," he said. Mom looked and discovered nothing.

Again, he said, "Look Mom."

I found myself staring at the most beautiful red fox—the size of a large Collie dog. He turned to wander off—majestically—and Chris only smiled a knowing smile. My thoughts went back to another setting—Richmond, Virginia—*Opera at the Mosque*—and all those antique furs, mostly red fox, out of storage for the occasion. Then the moment passed.

That evening, on our return home, Henry and daughter were waiting, and as usual, I tried to make interesting trips out of *incidentally* "beautiful scenery, heavy traffic, gorgeous sunsets," and, to me, the mere appearance of the handsome Fox.

After a lot of elaboration, and always some embroidery of the facts, Chris finally questioned me and remarked, "Oh Mom, stop carrying on so. It was only Francis Marion. He knew you were there and just stopped by to check on you!"

———◆◆———

DECEMBER 7, 1941—What were you doing on the Sunday afternoon of December 7, 1941? I think a book should be written and filled with those memories.

I was listening to the New York Philharmonic, always a treat. And this Sunday I was writing my letter of application for admission to the Woman's College of the University of North Carolina, in a town, unknown to me, by the name of Greensboro.

The shock of the newscast that day stilled my pen, and it was quite some time before I pulled myself, and my request, together. I was accepted and made plans to attend the late, great Woman's College of the University of North Carolina.

And followed thereafter four years of study and learning under very pleasant circumstances—concerned and helpful professors, wonderful concerts and lectures—plus a roommate who was comfortable and fun and who made being away from home acceptable.

———◆◆———

MORRISON NEESE—Showtime! Such a "Rustle of Spring," as presented once a year at the elegant emporium in downtown Greensboro, known only in memory as Morrison-Neese.

Located on Greene Street at the site of the present BB&T, it was seven floors of wonderful merchandise housed behind a slightly Venetian facade of yellow brick topped by elaborate cornice work. The builders of this structure obviously expected other high-rise buildings to join it on each side as these were faced with red brick.

I remember the 1940s: Every spring, two floors were completely redecorated to display new fashions in home furnishings, and the wealth of talent that created these designs. There was nothing else between Washington, with Woodward & Lothrop, and Atlanta, with W.E. Brown and Co., to compare with our establishment and its air of graciousness and good taste.

Clients and friends were invited by special cards announcing the occasion, and the public was informed by a full-page blow-up in the newspaper. Come and see! And in turn the germ of discontent was planted in the hearts and minds of housewives far and near—creating a desire for "that look" in their homes.

On the fifth floor, the rooms were decorated by Otto Zenke and his staff. Very special and elegant architectural backgrounds were his strong point. His designs in this field were executed by his brother Henry Zenke, and the finger work on beautiful handmade draperies was done by Margaret Thompson. Choice antiques and accessories were artfully displayed, creating the desire to just walk right in, sit down, and enjoy that room.

The second floor rooms-also newly refurnished—housed the most recently styled reproductions from North Carolina manufacturers and were the work of Mr. Ben Jones, of Hickory.

Fresh flowers, in great abundance, enhanced each room. They were massive, wonderful arrangements that I can only relate to White House style. These were created by the late Annie Fred Stafford Morton—and with such flair!

As the moment of "the opening" approached, things became as hectic as an opening night on Broadway. As visitors thronged into the building, pillows and draperies were being finished and patted into place, and paperhangers and painters were going out the back door.

Guests were received at the front door by eager staff members, then motored to the fifth floor by the elevator. The guests were allowed to walk down the five flights to enjoy the freedom of the entire store, for every inch was polished and arranged for viewing. All thirty employees had a part in this production and felt such a sense of pride in being involved. Dressed to perfection for the occasion, each one played the perfect host or hostess as if it were a manor house of his or her own.

And this is the memorable part—as each lady descended the stairs to the strains of very classical recorded music, she was given a beautiful, fresh white specimen gardenia which was pinned to her lapel for the occasion. There were thousands of them. One year the order was for three thousand blossoms—their scent permeating all seven floors of the building. Of course the occasion was enhanced by all the beautifully dressed and well groomed ladies and gentlemen, as it was a cultural event of some note in Greensboro. About eight-thirty in the evening, arrivals would slow down, and we would close, many of us moving on to the Carolina Theatre for a good movie.

The next day the crowds would start up all over again. The rooms were usually kept intact for a month before the furniture was sold, and the carpets and draperies remained in place until the next year at the same time.

This promotion developed some interesting results—mostly in the form of new customers and good sales for the rest of the year. Occasionally, someone would buy a whole room—as it was. I recall one very sweet lady—a nurse—who bought a pretty green and white boudoir. I also recall (and this is intriguing) that the housekeeper in the home where one decorator lived, would come and purchase only the designs of the other decorator—"fair Belinda."

What a place to work! Work? No—it was like living in a world of our own, where our energies were spent entirely on creating beautiful things and making people happy.

Never anything but fine appearances, backed-up by people who were good and thoughtful—and caring. There was no such thing as harassment—only encouragement to this young girl, just out of college at her first and, through the years, only job.

Is there any wonder that as summer approaches and the scent of gardenias wafts across the atmosphere that I am thrilled by the memory of it all?

What joy there is in waking up each day and wanting to go to work at that exciting place called Morrison-Neese!

As beautiful as the setting was, it sometimes paled in comparison to the interesting people who worked there. Mr. Morrison, the owner, became a legend in his own time in the furniture industry. He was the one who invited Otto Zenke to come to Greensboro. This move proved beneficial to both of them, and in time, Otto also became a legend.

Mr. Ben Jones returned to Morrison-Neese after the war and achieved success in his field. Mr. Herbert Wilson, bookkeeper and Citadel graduate, had very strict standards and ruled with an iron fist. It was always said that when you needed a new pencil, you had to turn in the stub of your old one! Mr. Barker, the manager, was seemingly very nice and pleasant. He could afford to be that way because his secretary was Mrs. Ellison who could absolutely curl your hair, and the curling iron was fear. She believed that never, ever, should you do anything on paper that required the use of the eraser on the pencil you had just picked up from Mr. Wilson.

There were upholsterers, ladies in the workroom who made beautiful draperies and slipcovers; carpet layers, and mechanics who could fix all the stoves and refrigerators; and an advertising department that made certain we were properly placed in the Sunday newspaper. There was Mr. Ray, in charge of a force of drivers who went from town to town making deliveries. Each day, two or three large trucks were loaded to make deliveries in North Carolina, South Carolina, and Virginia, as well as the deliveries in Greensboro.

In those days, Greensboro was a dry town. It took me quite a while to figure out why a big truck had to deliver at least one piece of furniture every Saturday to either Raleigh or Danville, not known as dry cities!

My favorite experience in those early years occurred when I had been there only a year-and-a-half. A nice looking couple walked in the front door (there was also an equally used back door) and asked to be helped. They wanted some advice about furnishing a home. Being unknown customers, the salesman of the day passed them along to me and told them I could give them all the advice they needed. As it turned out, it was furniture they needed, and lots of it. They had spent all of their lives living in hotels and owned nothing but a flat iron. Could I have their home ready to live in by Christmas? Five weeks to pull off a completely furnished home? Could I? I did! On Christmas Eve, we walked out with everything in place: carpets, draperies, complete rooms of furniture, accessories, bedding, linens, kitchen equipment, and even an ironing board! From that moment on, I was never content with my work unless it was as complete and perfect as that job. I knew what it was to experience the "job well-done."

At 5:30 P.M., on that Christmas Eve, a nice gentleman from High Point was waiting to drive me to my hometown where he was to visit his brother. My mother and father were waiting for their little girl, with a fire burning in the fireplace, and oysters broiling in the oven. A memorable Christmas.

On another occasion, in the fall, it was a dull Saturday afternoon, as many of the staff as possible had gone—guess where?—to a football game. Traffic was slow, but sure enough, in swished a beautifully dressed lady, armed with sables and a roll of house plans. She, too, would be wanting "advice" from a decorator! What to do? They were all gone. I was presented as such by the management and told to help her. What started out as a dilemma became a delight and a very productive experience. The lady lived in a small town in Eastern Carolina and became one of my best clients—sending me on to others in that part of the state. She had a lovely home that was like a nightclub, compared to the homes around her—mirrored walls, mahogany paneling and all. We became such good friends.

All of these things were learning experiences that rolled me along into being a decorator. Please let me explain my version of the terms "decorator" and "designer." I consider myself a designer who decorates. There, I said it! We heard, while visiting on the continent, that a "decorator" was a paper hanger or painter, and a great sigh of relief was expressed by Henry's relatives when they saw photos of our work in magazines. "Oh, thank goodness you are not decorators. You are what we call 'inner architects'"—a term whose use is forbidden in the United States for individuals in the business of interior design.

As complete as we liked to be with our jobs, sometimes something would go wrong—or almost wrong. We were installing a job in South Carolina, deep in the woods and swamps. The owner had highly placed relatives coming down to open the hunting season and wanted full use of the new home. Everything was in place except… guess what? About an hour before the guests arrived for a "social glass," our trucks rolled up with the eight sets of mattresses and box springs for the guest rooms! That was timing it a little close!

My memories include the beautifully decorated store windows, at Morrison Neese each one a complete room, ready for you to walk inside and get comfortable. And the Christmas windows were always so special. Otto and Henry Zenke would construct a fireplace that looked almost real, and the Christmas decorations were lovely. It was always fun to walk by as we went to the movies and listen to the comments of the "window shoppers." They were usually unaware of our identity and would speak honestly and make comments and take notes for their wish list for the future.

This good and working establishment eventually dissolved. Once the keystone of the operation pulled out, it went downhill rapidly, a sad ending. But the spirit was carried on by many of those people who were involved for a long while, and there is another generation of Zenkes, thank goodness!

1942—I had arrived in Greensboro, North Carolina to attend the late, great Woman's College of the University of North Carolina. Coming from the big city up in Virginia, I did not know what to expect. All shopping for clothes had been done at home where we had not only the intimate Naivette Shoppe, of long standing, but such grand emporiums as Smith & Welton and Ames & Brownley—all versions of Miller & Rhodes in Richmond and Lord & Taylor in New York, and with tea rooms.

Shock—shock—and more shock. Even though I had come to an inland town, I arrived to find a small, beautiful city and wonderful places to shop—silk stockings were still available here in 1942—long gone from my hometown.

It was not long before some magnet drew me directly to Montaldo's. The name itself sounded rhythmical and romantic, and the facade looked inviting.

The business had moved from quarters-up on the square in what I think was the ground floor of the Jefferson building. A local architect who went to New York and became very successful—Jack Coble—did over the new smooth-looking shoppe. Working with him, on interiors, was a native New Yorker who had come to Greensboro to later become very successful!— Otto Zenke.

Many years later I was to have the privilege of redecorating the stores in Greensboro and Winston-Salem, North Carolina.

Sleek and almost Hollywood was the style. Entering, one was surrounded by a beautiful setting. Lovely pieces of French furniture and boiserie set the stage for equally beautiful, lovely clothes. Soft pastel colors provided a wonderful background and did not compete with the merchandise. And a fragrance that was only Montaldo's enveloped customers as they entered. I was very lucky that my friend, who went in with me, introduced me to "her" saleslady—and lady she was—having come from an old family and having had, as well, her own private grand tour of Europe. She had a wardrobe of clothes (by then out of date, but not out of style) from the House of Worth in Paris designed and custom made just for her, and also sketches of the same. I remember seeing them and wanting to keep them. Alas—her clothes disappeared and *she threw out* those wonderful sketches.

Knowing someone like Louise Daniel (aka "Janie"), and dealing with one saleslady, assured the customer of instant service. The lady from the alterations room, Mrs. Wilson, also became used to the way of fitting that I required, and Mr. Lane always had fine shoes—and could fit my small, narrow foot! I was quickly and easily spoiled. It was all such a social event. Money did not change hands and was all handled through the mail.

Once, my mail was sent to my husband's office—a dangerous happening, so I asked Montaldo's bookkeeper to have the bills sent to her at the store. I then picked them up and took care of the matter, and our office force came to believe that I was not spending any money—thanks to Mrs. Carter.

The whole operation was pleasant—and spending money at Montaldo's was a joy! A bit of socializing—and I would usually see someone who wanted me to do some decorating. The fashion shows were glorious—worldly & elegant! And unneeded, but much admired, glamorous gowns and furs were sent down from New York for such occasions.

The day arrived when I needed the perfect wedding gown for the perfect groom and perfect wedding. I had always said I would not wear lace, but wear lace I did! And it was, indeed, perfect. Veil, shoes, and the trousseau to go with it—and the picture made at Montaldo's, sitting on that beautiful French sofa, covered in pale blue leather.

All through the years nothing was spared to make me feel comfortable and well dressed. And *I* was *not* the big spender in town. I was a career girl, but they knew that my appearance was "always Montaldo's."

Seven years after the beautiful wedding, our adorable princess was born, and guess where her playground was located? Two weeks after she was born, she was carried into Montaldo's on a pillow—for all to lo and behold! As she grew, she too, was spoiled. The ladies in the hat department at Montaldo's let her try on every hat she wanted to, whirling on the round-about stools. The cosmetic counter would be dusted and rearranged while I did my shopping—wonderful babysitting! And the day came when she would model for the fashion shows and also have her own wedding dress and trousseau. From Montaldo's, of course!

If one needed a different size or color of a dress or coat, telephone communication and orders would be filled, and overnight delivery was available for people who were in a rush. On trips to New York for our own business purposes, we would sometimes run into Mrs. Doop, the captain of this fleet of wonderful stores. Her sister, Nell Reed, who monitored everything and everyone in town, managed the Greensboro store. Later on, Bernice Bloom filled this role.

Back in 1957, Henry Zenke and I were traveling in England. We checked into a small hotel in Cambridge and went to the dining room for dinner. After we were seated, a couple came over and said, "You're from North Carolina aren't you?" They were from Charlotte and knew of us.

When asked how they knew we were from North Carolina, the reply was "That's easy, we saw the Montaldo's label on the coat lying in your car."

Once the famous and beautiful Jeanette MacDonald came to town for a concert—and while here, Montaldo's was asked to bring some evening gowns and dresses for her to try. It is not clear in my mind exactly how this was done—I think they were delivered to her hotel, the Sedgefield Inn. Miss Price was the saleslady who delivered them. Miss MacDonald's secretary was related to Irene Murphy in Greensboro. In any event, Miss MacDonald always sent word ahead to the Greensboro friend about the foods she would or would not eat—and to my knowledge Montaldo's did *not* make a sale to the Prima Donna.

The window displays—oh such gorgeously put together collections! And at Christmas they were spectacular. Shopping evenings for gentlemen at holiday times were most successful.

I recall, once, seeing in a window at the Winston-Salem store, a pink wool coat with a jewel mandarin collar—and *short sleeves*—only for Palm Beach. I did not buy it, but now, forty years later, I still think of it and want it. One outfit from Montaldo's was always more effective than a dozen others put together.

All the stores were like jeweled charms on a bracelet, scattered throughout the South and Midwest. They were "top drawer" in every way and definitely at the front of the retail business. Indeed, they made retailing a highly known and respected part of the community. They may have even been influential in advancing and stabilizing what became the field of interior decoration, ultimately making it prosper in the local world of trade.

It is all gone. I occasionally now gaze upon a Jacob Van Ruisdael painting of "A Cemetery." The name on one tomb is Montaldo. Did it die or was it killed? Mall outlets and catalogues should be sentenced for the crime.

———·•·———

MR. BLANDING'S DREAM HOUSE—A fun time for me, professionally, came when the book and, later the movie, *Mr. Blanding Builds His Dream House*, swept the country. Locally, the promotion was large and its publicity favorable.

A house under construction by a land owning company, a client who was ready to buy the house, a downtown emporium that was willing to supply the furnishings, and the blue ribbon girls from the local garden club who did very proper flower arrangements produced the ingredients to make this a real show. I do not know why I was selected to tie it all together as the decorator, except that the noted designers in the business had decided not to be a part of it.

Everyone made it easy for me, especially the clients who were purchasing the house. This was all speculation at its best, and on the Sunday afternoon of the opening, huge crowds appeared and continued through the weeks that followed.

This happening was a real send-off for an ingénue in this business.

———·•·———

1951—Henry returned from Christmas in New York and we made plans to attend a movie. As I waited for him to come, I heard bad news. Blue Bubble sirens. Oh no! I just knew Henry was getting a ticket for speeding! We were about to be late for the nine o'clock show and this would spoil everything for the evening. Sure enough, but we made it to the movie just in time.

Back home—we each reported of our separate visits home—and we both realized that these visits home would not suffice forever.

And Henry's words came forth: "Will you marry me?"

I did not say "yes." I did not say "no." I simply said, "When?"

The pleasure and the shock of the moment wore off and the conversation led to hopes and dreams. And Henry's first and foremost hope was to go back to Europe, a long trip. A trip to Europe! Thud! To Europe? Me? I was a little girl again, afraid of the water. I was still waiting for the Alcan Highway to be finished before considering a trip to Panama. And thinking only of my ancestors who made such an effort to get to America over almost four hundred years ago, why would I want to go back to Europe?

But we did, eventually, six years after the wedding. Prince Charming had appeared and, with his indulgence, I reclaimed some of Charleston. Henry Zenke fell right in with my love of the city and the state. We were married in St. Michael's at Christmastime in 1951 and honeymooned at 30 Meeting Street. The servants' quarters there had been turned into a lovely guest cottage. Mr. and Mrs. Dunn moved out their son and his guests so we could have the cottage. It was wonderful. I was actually living in Charleston!

The trip to Europe finally came to pass, the main purpose being to visit wartime sites. The airfield at Polebrook and Gloucester, where Henry had been stationed while in England, awaited our visit. Henry had the night shift at the weather station and would get in at about eight a.m., and his landlady would serve him his breakfast in bed. What a way to win a war. I met and enjoyed knowing the people he had talked about so much. They were like family to Henry. The Drinkwaters had two sons in school and Henry fit in just nicely.

I have a strong memory of the very cold weather that April. Guest rooms were single ones in the Drinkwater household, and one night it was so cold I had seven layers of what ever I could find for covers, and I was still cold.

Morning and time to dress, still freezing, I unashamedly went to the kitchen to dress by the stove—something I had only done while visiting my grandparents down south where central heat was seldom necessary. We had a fireplace in each room, but once in a while the weather would be freezing, so I would go to the kitchen and dress by the stove. Things were not so different in England from those in South Carolina.

———•◦•———

HOME AT 224 BLANDWOOD—Courtship with Henry was lovely and very proper. I, fortunately, lived with a loving and caring family, who enjoyed having me around to care for their children while they traveled whenever they wished.

Dates were movies, at least three times a week, and concerts. And I am so glad that we have the memory of those wonderful full-length features. Now we do not see three movies a year, much less three per week. And always chaperoned. Henry's brother was almost always in attendance. Afterwards we would retire to my "home," and under the watchful eye of my family, extend the evening. The proposal came just after the New Year in 1951. We had been "keeping company" for about four years.

One day as I walked around town looking for a house like the ones in Charleston, I came across what was visibly the worst looking house in town! But, it had good lines and good bone structure—long windows to the floor, a slate roof, square rooms, high ceilings, the original stairway with a mahogany banister, and six fireplaces. It even turned out to be older than I thought. The back part was a two over two-room house built in the earliest days of our town, about 1830. The front part, having been added by a man who had buried two wives by 1849, also had some age.

Once we saw what a good skeleton it was, we became excited about making it our home. Could we buy it? No. It was part of an entailed estate belonging to some friends of Henry. They finally agreed to lease it to him at a monthly rate, with purchasing available at the end of ten years. Money to restore it? Absolutely none was available at the banks. Preservation and restoration was not recognized as a profitable thing to do or be involved with, not in this town, anyway. Location was everything and this was in the "wrong" part of town, surrounded by city and county government buildings. Pluses: it was in the neighborhood of one old house called Blandwood, the home of Governor John Motley Morehead, and we could almost make it look like a home in Charleston! So Henry leased it. This was several months before the wedding.

One day, at work, one of my fellow employees approached the delicate subject of, "When are you and Henry going to get married"?

I really did not have an answer because we had just imagined that we would slip off one day to St. Michael's in Charleston to be married. (I have never been able to figure out how anyone "slips off" to anywhere to get married!) But back to my fellow employee:

"You know what people are saying about you, Virginia?"

"No. What?"

"That you won't marry Henry because he hasn't found a house good enough to suit you in the Park." (The Park was the high rent district of our town.)

This was the very day that Henry had signed the papers to lease the old, run down, dilapidated structure in the "wrong" part of town that waited to be my Charleston house! The results were published in *House Beautiful*, September 1964, for you to see.

———•◆•———

IMAGINATION—Imagination is such a part of "doing history." We have not actually seen history's cast of characters. We were not there to behold their customs or the way they lived. Letters and written accounts of verbal encounters can only create a setting for us to imagine—to believe.

Such was the situation in Charleston, one night in the early 1950s. While visiting there on the occasion of our wedding anniversary, Henry Zenke and I attended an event at the Heyward-Washington House. The arrival of George Washington was to be reenacted—and reenacted it was! We were almost late and the only seats left were at a front window seat in the upstairs drawing room. All was by candlelight and standing out in my memory is the beautiful chimneypiece in that room—and pleasant chatter. We were all waiting for the arrival of "George Washington!" Soon, the approach of a carriage was heard, the clip-clop of the horses, the squeaking of the carriage, and I looked out of the window and down on the white wig of someone portraying the "Father of Our Country." I was stilled! Was it? Could it be? It was all so real. Shortly, the sound of footsteps on the stair quieted the chatter, and from where I sat, the shadow of the figure coming up the stairs could be seen quite clearly. Remember the candlelight! My heart kept time with the studied steps of our hero. I saw his shadow. I believed. Delusions that George Washington was appearing, to all of us in that room, became very real. And to me, he *was* George Washington! Good casting and good candlelight! It was all very convincing. And Virginia and, I think, Henry felt frozen in time. It is such a memory now a half of a century old.

A reception downstairs, also by candlelight, did not dampen my firm belief that George Washington, himself, had been with us. A host couple helped to continue our pleasure by inviting us home with them for a visit.

We always felt welcome in Charleston.

———— ·•·•· ————

A. EISENSTAEDT—Among the many trips to Charleston, there is one that stands out in my memory. Having been married there, it was a pattern in our lives for us to go there as often as possible.

Several years after our daughter was born, the Zenkes were called upon to do work at the Citadel. I was not involved, but I was thrilled at the idea. Henry went down to start the job, and then I attended when we went back to install the work. It was interesting, working with the military mind—Mark Clark to be specific. Everything had to be down on paper and then carried out according to plan, no revisions as you go along. How did we win World War II?

During the day, while Henry was working, Ginia and I had fun. We got dressed up (Charleston bonnet and gloves for her) and went riding around in Captain Wagner's horse-drawn carriage. At that time, his was the only such accommodation in town. I could think of nothing finer than to ride around with him, looking at Charleston, but discussing his Vienna. The best of my two worlds.

As we rode around the city, we were aware of tourists and photographers. Among them was my close friend and historian, Sam Stoney (Samuel Gaillard Stoney, architect and historian). He waved to us several times. We waved back and kept on going.

The next day, we continued our drives and Henry was able to join us. As we went down Meeting Street, there was Sam Stoney and party again. We waved, and this time he blocked our path and just stood there while we halted.

"Dear Lady Virginia," Sam said. "Will you pause long enough to accommodate me and let this gentleman take your picture?"

Flattery got him everywhere, though I could not understand what was behind it.

"Why yes, Sam. What do you want us to do?" Virginia asked.

"Just ride slowly and look at the architecture," Sam replied.

"But Sam, that's what I've been doing all day," I said.

Aside, Sam finally enlightened me.

"My dear, this gentleman is Alfred Eisenstaedt from *LIFE*. We have been trying to get you on film for two days. Just be still!"

"Yes sir," I responded.

Some thirty or forty shots were taken of the Zenkes riding around Charleston for *LIFE* magazine. Our one picture appeared in the magazine several months later. It looked good if you had a magnifying glass!

This man was the photographer of presidents, movie stars, and famous sportsmen. The kiss of a sailor and a girl in Times Square on the day of Victory—World War II—was, I think, made by him. A recent newspaper announced Alfred Eisenstaedt's death. We were honored to be among his subjects.

We still occupied quarters on the second floor of our home, an apartment with an upstairs sitting room. Our little daughter was only about three years old. We had no television set, so our time after dinner was spent reading and playing with toys, so many toys. Everyone who came to visit brought a treat of some kind to Ginia. Usually it was some small gift that she could hold in her hand, and know that it was her very own property.

Alas, one evening as we were thus engaged, Ginia started crying for no obvious reason.

I convinced her to stop crying, but eventually said, "Why are you crying? What is wrong?" Through the weeps came distinguishable words, "I've got a little man up in my nose!"

"I don't believe it, now stop crying," which only brought forth more wailings.

Henry's lack of sympathy made me think she was making it up. I glanced at the floor, and scattered about was one of her recent gifts, a group of little men stacked into one larger man, covered each other, and one was missing….

When it all came together in my mind, I could only scream, "She does have a little man up her nose!"

At this point, Henry conceived that I, too, had lost my mind. Calling the doctor—back then you could still communicate with them after hours—and he had a hard time understanding me, but Dr. Wilson said to get her to his office. Henry was convinced by this time! When we arrived, he was waiting for us, and, with all assurance and composure, removed the article from her nose. It was indeed the missing little man. Suppose we had not believed her or suppose, suppose…

FAMILIARITY—We were traveling to a part of our country that I had never visited. We were on our way to Milwaukee to visit my sister and her family. I had never been west of the Mississippi and, certainly, never to Chicago and beyond.

Our three-year-old daughter was with us and she was weathering the trip rather well, except she had lost her appetite. We stopped mostly at short order places for the first two days and she would only shake her head and refuse to eat.

Then we arrived in Lexington, Kentucky, and while there planned to eat at the Country Club which had been decorated by Ginia's uncle and company. She walked into very familiar surroundings, felt quite at home, and ate everything in sight.

Familiarity in this case only bred acceptance and comfort!

CLIENTS—If it sounds as if all clients were perfect, that is an error. And if it sounds as if I was perfect, that too is an error. If there is one thing I have learned about being a decorator, it is the fact that you can only do what the client will let you do. Period! Absolutely!

The perfect situation is to give a client an overview of what you would like to do with color, (that is the most sensitive area), and have them say, "Give me a ball park figure," and then have them say, "Don't bother me until you are finished." Usually a dreamboat of a job, executed with a minimum of time wasted, and, therefore, saves money in the process. The difficult ones drag it out with too much conversation. The worst ones keep asking, "Isn't there something better?" or, "Are you sure?" Yes, there is always something better, next year and the year after that. And yes, I am sure or I would not have said so in the first place!

In all these years, there have only been three or four people I could not deal with, and I simply had to back away from those situations because I was unable to get a real reading. Perhaps they had to back away from me because in, and through me, they expected solutions to problems that went beyond material things. I harbor guilt about failure in these circumstances, but not much.

Like doctors, we have to study the patient and once we know how they live and operate a household, we can prescribe. In certain circumstances, the house, and a proper interpretation of it, has become more important to me than the likes and dislikes of the client. That, however, cannot always be solved as easily as it seems. Patience is often required to guide clients through the maze of a production. That's what it is, a production! I even refer to some of my verbal solutions as Sunday school lessons. Like doctors, we are on call, day and night, and should be. We are here to help. And, if talking to me late at night or weekends makes one more comfortable, so be it.

While the telephone is a great invention, it can become what I call the black devil. Indeed, there have been times in the past when I knew who was calling before I picked up the receiver, and this was prior to caller ID. There were a few clients (not of mine but of others) who were always heard from on the "full of the moon" and "Mondays after" were unbelievable.

<hr>

Three large moving vans sat in the driveway of a new residence, full of new furnishings, carpet, draperies, and accessories. "The best laid plans…" It snowed, a good heavy snow and there the vans sat, waiting to be unloaded. Beautiful house, nice job, and wonderful clients.

Once we could get in, things went smoothly. When everything fits and matches, all is well.

Toward the end of the installation, which took at least three days, there was some small piece of furniture that I thought would look better if it were painted black. Painters were still on the job, so it was "no problem."

Want to bet?

The painter took the item to the basement and painted it quickly. The heating system was on and forcing air throughout the house! Air and a fine layer of black paint spread throughout the house, and all over the white silk draperies and white wool carpet.

Decorator panicked—that's me. I put a call in to my hero, dear Henry, and after he quieted me down, simply said, "Virginia, be quiet and listen. Do not touch it. Let it dry and then vacuum everything."

House cleaners came in and did just that and nobody could tell that this disaster had happened!

Happy ending? Yes.

———•◆•———

Doing work for interesting people often times resulted in my receiving some unusual thoughts:

A client, whose wife was very short while he was quite tall, sent me the following poem, which he wrote while I did work for them:

The McLeans were having a bit of a quarrel

(Nothing naughty, nothing immoral)

It simply seems that neither spouse

Could agree on redecorating the house.

So they called in an interior decorator

To act as sort of arbitrator

This decorator, Virginia Zenke

Was pretty crafty, pretty slinky.

Said she, these pictures should hang a bit higher

And Tom just nodded, but Itty caught fire

Said Itty, Virginia can go to the devil

These pictures will hang at *my* eye level!

But Virginia's crafty, and from a big City

And will recommend elevator shoes for Itty.

These are the types of things that can never be figured in the price of doing a job because they *are* so priceless.

CASTING BREAD—As an aftermath of some of our large, successful jobs, I would be asked, as a favor to the client, to help or advise a friend in the same town—usually someone of modest means, but who still liked nice things. If this could take place while we were making deliveries to that town anyway, it was no hardship, and the management approved. Hardship? No, it was a challenge.

My client and friend with the sables and show house was a wonderful and down-to-earth person. One would never have known that her clothes were custom-made. Designers would come to her from far away to give her showings. Her shoes were also custom-made and with her name inside. There was always a new outfit for each and every occasion. I had come from a large city, but there were moments when I thought living in a small town might be a good substitute!

My friend with the sables wanted me to help her dear friend decorate her very small house. The big job had cost many, many times the amount of money involved in the smaller job, but how could I say no? The nice small house was already furnished, but not "decorated," so we began. We changed the wallpaper in two rooms, made draperies for another room, slip-covered a sofa, put curtains on French doors, found lamps and accessories, and voila! In 1951, the bill was less than $800.00.

Now you may think that was not profitable, but one never knows when one is casting bread upon the waters, for it all came back to me in the most rewarding way.

The happy client awarded me some sort of sainthood for making her little home so lovely, and thereafter we had special places in our hearts for each other.

Now this small town was one of many small towns along Highway 301, wending slowly through North Carolina. My mother, who lived in Virginia, would take this route to visit her relatives in South Carolina.

My mother has always reserved an area of suspicion about my work.

"Why don't you go to work at the same time every morning? Why don't you get home at the same time every evening? Why do you work on Saturday?"

And God knows what she would think if she knew I spent time on Sunday, working out my thoughts. (I am ashamed to even think of the number of rooms I have decorated while in a church pew, especially when the acoustics are bad and the delivery dull.) So if mother went to South Carolina, she also returned on Highway 301. Traveling with her on this one occasion was a friend; and, as they were wending their way back toward Virginia, this friend said, "Let's stop and see my friend who lives in the next little town."

"Fine." Mother was, and always has been, a great visitor. So they stopped to see the friend, who turned out to be the lady with the small house that had been decorated by somebody named Virginia Ford. Guest was Mrs. Ford, and a good time was had by all. My sainthood was embellished by mother's host and hostess. The bread I had cast upon the water had returned as strawberries on shortcake with whipped cream, floating in champagne. I have never had such a glowing letter from my mother! And if you don't believe there is a Supreme Being up there after that, I do! Years of my seeking parental approval were washed away with this accidental visit.

When I finally watched the movie *Steel Magnolias*, I felt very akin to that situation by way of that lovely small town. The enormous difference in material wealth throughout the community, and the fact that such wealth, or lack thereof, did not affect the richness of friendships.

⸺ ⋅◆⋅ ⸺

MINDING THE STORE—I think we sometimes know when we are casting bread upon the waters.

We were ready to leave town on a trip and a call came from acquaintances who needed help, and needed it before we were to leave. Advice was the only commodity involved, so I made a short visit to advise. Suggestions brought forth a degree of opposition, and I left somewhat frustrated. The only sale that resulted was a small order for some light fixtures.

Fixtures were ordered, delivered, and billed. About a month later, our very efficient bookkeeper announced that the bill for the items had not been paid and that she was sending another one. I suggested that she not do this, as they were friends of friends and would pay eventually.

Misfortune is a terrible thing and, as I later found out, it had descended on this client. Doubled in spades. Time passed and the bookkeeper suggested sending another bill. I said, "NO." She insisted, "YES."

She accused me of being unprofessional and told me that I did not know how to run a business. So that may be. I simply do not have the instincts of a shopkeeper. Further threats made me finally pull rank, and I told her absolutely not to send any more bills regarding this matter.

Time passed. About a year later, we received a check with a lovely note, thanking us for our patience in the matter!

End of story?

No! About another year later, a call from the same client asked if we felt like helping them with some work at their home. We agreed to consider it, and they followed up by letting us do over the entire house, and the expense was considerable.

Thoughtfulness takes so little effort and can be so rewarding.

————•◆•————

TIME TO INSTALL—Moving time is always a touchy situation no matter how much planning one does. Something can go wrong and usually does.

We planned in November for installation, specifically on January 12, and guess what? It snowed on the eleventh. No matter. The client was what I can only call willful, and we moved her in with the snow. Up to the sixth floor of what, in our town, was a high rise.

Into the same apartment complex, we moved another client. Such special things we did for her. There were two adjacent closet doors in a narrow hallway. And we built a shallow façade to make them look like a piece of French furniture. Bathtubs were not deep enough to suit her, so we constructed one, of beautiful tiles, that was deeper, and I have a strong memory of Rosie and Henry getting into it to check the depth. First one, and then the other, of course, for it was a very small tub. She was the only client who even let me cover up the always-misplaced thermostat. Never located in the center of the wall, always where they will show. Of course I realize there is a reason for this arrangement, but it never pleases me. A small carriage clock with its works removed was the answer. It sat upon a small wall shelf, to be easily moved when the thermostat needed adjusting. If it ever messed up the heating arrangement, I never heard.

White wall-to-wall carpet went into the small kitchen. I was so embarrassed by this that when the order was placed with the manufacturer, I definitely neglected to say, "mark the shipment 'kitchen.'"

Things went smoothly the day we moved in, until the moment we tried to get up to the ninth floor with a large breakfront. Its being in three pieces did not help. There was no way up but to take it up outside the building and onto a balcony, and then into the apartment. Henry put a jack on the roof and up it went.

The funny side of this story regards the funeral home located across the street. Such an audience we had. Were they expecting some sudden business out of that operation? Being queasy and six months pregnant, I was ordered not to watch. Successfully in place and to be admired by all, the breakfront made the room, and the staff across the street went back to reading the obituaries.

⸻ ◦ ◦ ◦ ⸻

FOLGER LIBRARY—All jobs are interesting, but occasionally one presents itself and develops into something more challenging and more rewarding than others. Such a one was the chance to do some renovation at the Folger Library in our nation's capital. Devoted to memorabilia of the English Bard, Shakespeare, it housed an enormous collection of his works and artifacts.

The opportunity to do some work there came from a friend who was assistant to the then director, and he felt that we were the ones to do the job.

Consultation on sight was very interesting. We met with the Director and with Mrs. Folger, and had lunch in the rooms we were to improve. Things went well, except the Director liked Swedish modern furniture and that did not please me. Mrs. Folger was very understanding and the result was that it would be done my way.

All of this was underground. Large vaults for more storage space were being created to house more books. Our work involved a large lecture and meeting room, comfortable for that purpose and also to be used as a reception area. An adjoining room was a tearoom. No problems. The library owned many pieces of antique furniture, and quite a collection of nice paintings. All were made available for my use on this project.

It actually worked out very well considering the many posts, acting as large supports, in the room. Henry did a lovely arch to conceal the movie screen for the projection of slides. The screen came down from behind the arch and the mechanics were all concealed, not spoiling the appearance of the reception room.

One very interesting thing happened while at that great library. I could use anything they had in storage in the way of paintings, accessories, and furniture, but I could not use any of their books for display purposes. I had to buy books elsewhere to place in the lecture room!

Mrs. Folger was very pleased with the outcome!

While doing this work, we were housed in a guesthouse of some vintage, comfortable enough and very convenient. Installation time meant that we would be there for at least three or four days to complete the set-up of everything.

I found myself getting up and going down into the job site while it was still very dark, and remaining there throughout the day, leaving well after dark. Lunch was brought in each day so I did not see daylight for the working period of several days. My staff and others followed the same pattern except that they would get out of doors to run errands of various sorts.

Several days later we finally left, after dark, to drive home. I wanted to get home that night. A long, six-hour drive followed. At one point we were close to our farm and could have stopped there. "No," I said. I wanted to get home to Greensboro. When we arrived, we fell into bed, exhausted.

I think people do not realize what a drain these productions can be. They take energy out of you just as a performance on stage would do. And after sleeping for an hour or two, something happened that I had never before experienced. I woke up screaming, sat upright in bed, and screamed for several minutes. No nightmare, just screaming. Henry finally calmed me, but then could not stop my crying.

What had happened? I will never know. Was I traumatized—reacting to being underground without daylight for so long?

I pity all those people who work in offices without windows, and who are enclosed daily. Surely it affects their personalities. I recovered but was a bit shaken by the experience.

———•◆•———

AIKEN, SOUTH CAROLINA—Six hundred invitations had been mailed out to announce the opening of a new club in Aiken, South Carolina for a Friday evening. Stacks of boxes, containing chairs and other furniture, filled the rooms to be decorated. They had been drop-shipped directly to the site and had to be unboxed. Our company trucks rolled up on Wednesday evening before the event. The manager was in a rage. There was no way, he thought, that he could receive his 600 guests in forty-eight hours. Little did he know of how we operated. Many truckloads of furniture and accessories were unloaded by our crew of four, plus Henry, me, and our two children (it was their spring break from school). What hard work and what fun they had watching that monster of a building take form and be shaped into a lovely clubhouse.

Late on Thursday night, we had to put together an entire room to be photographed for the newspapers, immediately dismantle it so the walls could be painted the right color, and then put it back together. At 6:00 P.M. on Friday, we walked out of the back door as the cream of up-country South Carolina society streamed through the front door. Everything was in place, including a shining and proud manager. At the end of the reception line of six hundred, the meek, mild, and grateful Zenkes walked in the front door, elegantly attired, to find themselves being hugged and kissed by the manager, who had not spoken to them for 48 hours! That was an Easter vacation my children will never forget.

———•◆•———

PUT-DOWNS—A properly presented put-down can be a "thing of beauty and a joy forever!" A great occurrence of balance, I even laugh when I am the one who is put down.

One Christmas season, an educated and well-traveled friend stopped by for a glass of cheer and a visit. It was sort of an annual event and it had been a long time between visits.

Right off, he said, "Well, Virginia, I know you have been busy, so tell me what you have been up to!"

"Oh my, work, work, and more work. A nice job out of town, trips to the farm, 'exciting?'" Trips to High Point, et cetera. And now, tell me what you have been up to."

"Well, my dear, two weeks ago tonight I was having dinner with Prince Charles at Highgrove!"

Thud. How much more down can you be put than that? I loved it.

On one occasion when we were house touring in Maryland, another put-down came to pass.

One of the most gorgeous houses in the United States is on the bay near Annapolis. It is not advertised or written about and is generally unavailable to the public eye. It is a lovely mid to early eighteenth century house that had been painstakingly restored to its original splendor. And splendid it was! Removal of nineteenth century columns took it back to its original form, that of a glowing pavilion. Being with the Society of Architectural Historians for their annual meeting that year, we were privileged to see this glorious reconstruction and restoration of Whitehall. Impressed to speechlessness I was!

And while there in a room crowded with people that included the owner, I witnessed one of the finest of put-downs to come my way. I love a good put-down. We had counted something like almost a dozen Chinese Chippendales over mantels throughout the house, and while standing in a room filled, chair rail to ceiling and over doors, with portraits of George Washington, The Lees, Randolphs, Carters, and most likely some Harrisons, etc.; on and on, wall to wall they hung to the ceiling.

The owner of the house was graciously present and answered questions generously.

I stood near enough to hear the following conversation between a guest and the owner:

"Where in the world did you locate all these wonderful portraits of these important people?"

The owner replied, "They came with my family. I inherited them all!"

Ouch! How I loved that classy put-down and was ever so grateful that I had not asked the question myself!

———◦•◦———

MY CHURCH—Many years of being allowed to help keep my church beautiful has added to my pleasure and, sometimes, heartache. I always felt that I was imposing on the vestry by trying to keep things beautiful, and useful, as well. Why is it that clients will spend hundreds of thousands of dollars and never complain, but you cannot make a gift of anything to committee members without intense questioning?

Our budget was such that I felt we were holding things together only by faith (i.e. chewing gum and scotch tape).

This situation finally broke when some newcomers informed the membership that the church needed to be fixed! This brought forth the terror on my part (recalling the budgets for chewing gum and scotch tape!).

We did fix the church and they did let me help, and my children afforded the beautiful book of memorials created for us by Don Etherington, Conservator.

One incident many years before—the death of a member brought forth great generosity on the part of a parent. The chapel needed work, and funds were offered for this. My question was, how much was I allowed to spend?

The reply from the parent was, "Virginia, you may spend any amount you need or want to as long as so-and-so and so-and-so have nothing to do with the project. I do not want them to have anything to say or be involved in any way with these happenings!"

Was I ever elevated? The unnamed were two members who criticized everything, and tried to run church, social clubs, and society in general.

It is still the same beautiful, with continued care, chapel as it was many years ago.

TO THE TRADE ONLY—Being a decorator on occasion provokes resentment. Volunteering to help without charge is not always appreciated. Why is it that a client who is spending many thousands of dollars will accept every suggestion, but the person or group benefiting from free advice stops you dead in your tracks as you try to help them for free?

The furnishings committee had to meet, and was to approve a plan to refurbish a public room. The donor of the gift was present at the meeting and announced loud and clear that he did not want me involved, that he, in fact, wanted "to be the decorator." He further announced that he and his advisor had spent hours and days seeking out suitable furnishings, available at the High Point Furniture Market. More hours and days were spent touring these facilities, supposedly "open to the trade only." Final decisions were made with the approval of the committee and myself, and the orders were placed by the generous benefactor. Surprise!!! He learned, to his horror, that the orders for his project had to go through—guess what?—a local decorator who handled the products. Guess who that was? Right!—They were such good sports about this transaction.

WHOLESALE CLIENTS—My bête noire is to get involved with clients who can get furniture wholesale! Usually we find out before we start a job if this is the case and do not continue.

Furious is what I am when we have made suggestions for a plan and then have the client say, "I can get it wholesale."

Our profits are made from selling merchandise at a retail price suggested by the manufacturer. And we do not charge for advice. We expect to sell the customer what is needed to do the job.

That I am able to buy items occasionally for personal use can also be a problem. I had never selected china and crystal patterns at the time of my wedding. So one day we were at 225 Fifth Avenue, that fantastic emporium for "getting it wholesale." Into a well-known showroom of crystal I thought, oh my, now is the time. After much deliberation, I selected a pattern and proceeded to purchase a dozen of each glass and items that were made all to match.

They all arrived well packaged, and horror of horrors, I realized that I did not have a place to store these items. Encased, the boxes took up a small room, floor to ceiling.

I then told shipping to return them as soon as possible.

Big boss was horrified. He was one of their best clients and did not want to be out of favor by returning such a large order.

"How can you not keep them? What will I tell them about your actions?"

Simple, "Tell them I died."

And to this day my table is often set with mismatched vessels.

———•◆•———

Compliments, while not given often, are forever welcome; and never more so than when they come from a relative or someone close.

A wedding in the family always brings out the best of endeavors from the mother of the bride. And, of course, we rose to the occasion in order to get that accomplished.

Putting forth our best efforts created a new look to a tired library den and with a blooming spring outside, the inside seemed to glow. It was as if the whole room looked new.

As we were almost ready to walk out, the bride-to-be said, "Maybe we should call Dad and let him see how it looks." Dad was home for the afternoon and reading in his upstairs office, so it was no inconvenience to get him to appear.

Such a transformation had taken place. And when he walked in, all he could say was, "My goodness, it looks like Christmas morning!" And my wonderful daughter, standing by, quickly said, "Yes, Santa Claus, there is a Virginia!"

Such a compliment.

———•◆•———

Compliments come in different forms, not always verbal. One day I was scheduled to go to a meeting, a committee meeting, and the babysitter who was due could not be with us, so I took my four-year-old son with me. The meeting consisted of about ten women and they all smiled questioningly at this young one in attendance.

At their morning meetings, soft drinks were usually served about mid-morning, but on this occasion, it was thought that it would keep the young visitor quiet and occupied by serving him his Coke immediately. The hostess called Chris over to pick up his drink. Across the room he walked, was handed his glass, and across the room he walked back, straight to me. In his mind, his mother was to be served first. Such a gentleman at that early age and such a compliment.

———•◦•———

COMPLIMENTS CONTINUED—While attending the Antiques Forum in Williamsburg one year, I endured what I consider quite a compliment.

The Forum always opened with a cocktail party, usually on a Sunday night. While meeting and greeting other guests, my party was engaged in conversation, and an awareness of my name and presence brought forth the usual minor stroke on the part of another guest. Recognition of the name I bear brought on the usual gasps. Oh! Ooh! Oooh! Are you related? Excitement over being in the presence of someone who actually breathed air in the same room with The Great One eventually died down, and we returned to pleasant conversation.

The final comment of another guest was, to me, very flattering.

"For all the beautiful rooms you all create, I must say that you know when to stop embellishing. You know when to leave things out. You know when to simplify. You know when to quit."

Now, that is, indeed, a compliment.

———•◦•———

COMPLIMENTS 4—Being involved with the Preservation and restoration brought us into contact with many people of note. Among them was the late Clem Conger, curator of the reception rooms at the State Department. And oh, was he persuasive, and what a wonderful job he did of talking people into allowing their heirlooms to be displayed to enhance those rooms, and how marked an improvement they made! My first visit there left me having only dismal thoughts of the impressions that must have been forever created in the eyes of visiting diplomats.

There was an occasion for Mr. Conger and his wife to visit our Tarover while touring the area and other old houses. It was his favorite approach, to locate something—furniture or paintings that might be relevant regarding the history of our country—a mirror, painting, or a piece of something related to our founding fathers. He would then enforce his gentle persuasion and then the item would be gifted or loaned for his project. I felt he had learned a lot from Queen Mary, wife of George V. It has provided me with much amusement remembering his visit to Tarover. As he was leaving, Clem stated that he could safely say that this was the only historic house he had ever visited from which he did not want to take anything home. Having furnished this big country house with leftovers and early attic contents, I loved his remarks!

COMPLIMENTS FOR HENRY—One of the most complimentary and flattering occurrences happened to Henry Zenke. We were working in a new house, out of town, for a family by the name of Meech. All of the interior woodwork had been designed by Henry. Each room was fitted out to perfection with beautifully detailed touches, including very thin drawers—wide enough to include such things as maps. Imagine our reaction when, upon completion, these very drawers housed the beautiful, full-scale, detailed drawings that my husband had done for them. And the pleasure our clients experienced when they opened these cases to display the drawings. Henry was, indeed, very flattered.

ANCESTRY—Bride from down south, groom from up north—was this to be trouble down the road? I hoped not. Henry's European background mitigated the situation. Although his grandfather had served in the Grand Army of the Republic, he did not emphasize this part of his background. And his favorite general in blue was General Thomas, a Southerner from

Virginia who remained loyal to the Union.

In most discussions, he understood and sympathized with the South. So, there was seldom any serious discussion about the War Between the States, especially after the children arrived. We wanted no division of thought in their minds. We were American, pure and simple.

Our travels took us through many states on the east coast and one weekend found us in Lexington, Virginia. We were fascinated with architecture that was designed by A. J. Davis at Virginia Military Institute and loved the campus at Washington and Lee University.

We were about to end our tour and were close to the chapel there, so I said very pleasantly, "Henry, we really should go in and view the recumbent Robert E. Lee."

My very young son come forth with the query, "Who is Robert E. Lee?"

Shock! His mother realized how neglectful she had been.

This pattern followed through World War I when Henry's German relatives opposed my relatives in that conflict! Never, ever did we tell my father about that connection or that Henry was of German descent. We have taught the children to respect the good of both ancestries. World War II discolored that, and by this time all consideration was for Americans first!

Guess what dinner conversations were about after that!

———•◦•———

1996—Having arrived at the Ritz Carlton Buckhead the night before, I happily went to the club for breakfast at a leisurely 9 A.M. My sense of well-being and complacency manifested itself in my having coffee and reading the *Atlanta Constitution*. The weather was dreadful—heavy rain, and I felt no sense of urgency to get out and to work, if going to the Atlanta Decorative Arts Center (ADAC) is work. For me, it is fun.

Local news I read first, having Atlanta connections generations ago, so I found myself reading the obituaries. And there, staring me in the face in bold headlines was the name of my first cousin—deceased and to be buried at 10:00 A.M., less than an hour later, and miles away in Decatur, Georgia. We had not been close for many years, but she was my mother's favorite niece, so I felt that I should attend the services. I told my son that I had to go to a funeral and would see him later. I went downstairs to the lobby, and spoke to the bell captain to explain that I needed a car and a driver now!

"You must speak to the concierge," was his reply.

The minutes ticked away. I explained my plight to the gentleman at the desk and got this response:

"Mrs. Zenke, it will take me at least an hour to locate a car and driver for you. With this rain, we are very busy."

And at that very moment someone touched my elbow.

"Mrs. Zenke, I have a car waiting for you if you will step outside. The driver is waiting to take you wherever you want to go!"

Miracles do happen. I stepped into a long limousine and a very considerate and gentlemanly driver asked my destination.

"Decatur," I replied.

"Where in Decatur?" he asked

"The old cemetery."

"And what is the address?"

By now it was 9:35 A.M., and he spent at least five minutes trying desperately, even calling his wife, to find out the address of the cemetery.

"Please, sir, I must be there by 10:00 A.M. Please hurry."

At 10:02 A.M., we rolled into my destination. I immediately went to the family car, spoke to my relatives all with Marvin, who held an enormous umbrella over my head. Then we went through a lengthy Southern graveside service, cold and wet, but my driver stayed with me the whole time. He then took me back to Atlanta and my appointment with my son at ADAC.

I wonder who's "driving Miss Daisy" somewhere this week… I hope it's Marvin's Peachtree Sedans.

As always, the Ritz Carlton at Buckhead was thoughtful and caring. Many years earlier when I was staying there and my son was only about twelve years old, I was elsewhere and asked all the help to keep me informed of his whereabouts. And one afternoon I returned to my room to find a note. "Mrs. Zenke, your son is on the second floor of Saks, talking to a blond! 3:45 P.M." Such service!

1943 CLASSROOM—Shaking with fear! I had been told by my new art teacher to draw shoes—page after page of line drawings of shoes, but only old shoes—with character. Alas, I had just been sent off from Virginia to North Carolina with only new shoes!

1963, LIFE AFTER CLASSROOM—Rejoicing with a sense of accomplishment, heretofore unknown, when I was asked by the acting head of the department of art to return to the college to teach! Teach what? How to transfer loving beauty (art) into creating beauty (art) for others to enjoy?

It has been my very good fortune to be able to transform an unknowing and seemingly untalented student, myself, who was unable to put beauty on paper, into a force for creating surrounding forms of beauty. Helen Thrush is one of several people along this path of creativity who helped me to accomplish what became my goal. One day, long after graduation, I received a letter from her, asking Henry and me to help her turn her home into a "jewel box," and it was one of the most complimentary requests to ever come my way. We can only do what people let us do—and Helen Thrush did just that—she let us do what we wanted to do in order to arrive at what became a bit of visual and usable perfection. All went well until she wanted whipped cream on the cream that had already been whipped. I could do no more, and I can say no more than that Helen Thrush has been a very strong implement in helping me to be the creative person I wanted to be—and am.

And, Miss Thrush, I finally got to Budapest—but did not find your "Black Prince" whom you dated. (Of course I did not look very hard—I already had Prince Henry.)

Please know that my children and I will always cherish the two precious "peacock spoons" you so generously gave us from your family. After much research we learned that the "WM" or "MW" was the touch mark of not one, but two silversmiths working in Philadelphia between 1790 and 1805, Christian *Wilberger* and Will *Mannerback*.

J. FATH/HELEN'S—Having sparked an interest in that wonderful emporium known as Morrison-Neese has brought forth inquiries and comments on other events that, perhaps, should be expanded upon as I recall them.

Always, people would ask if Mr. Morrison is still living—no; and what happened to Mr. Neese, who apparently dropped out of the act very early in the development of the business? The other question is always, "When did Otto come to Greensboro?" and, "When did his brother Henry come to Greensboro?"

Otto arrived in Greensboro about 1937, and Henry arrived in 1946, after having served in the air force in Europe in World War II.

Life in Greensboro, at that time, was very interesting. It was just after the war and business was beginning to pick up in the furniture world.

While recently reading one of the "elite" magazines of September 1994, an advertisement appeared that caught my eye and brought back memories. The house of Jacques Fath has apparently been reconstructed and reinstated among the couture houses of Paris. Clothes of elegant simplicity were his designs of the late 1940s and early 1950s.

I was certainly surprised one day, while sitting at my desk to look up and see Jacques Fath himself wandering around Morrison-Neese. This was in 1951. He was trim, very nice-looking and polite, dressed as I remember in gray slacks and a black turtleneck sweater—simply elegant.

During his visit, there was an occasion to have dinner at the Embassy club, and when my intended and I arrived, the place was packed. If you could get on the dance floor, you might not be able to get off of it. It must have been during the Furniture Market because the Embassy club (aka Helen's) was the favorite local watering hole of the furniture business. Henry and I rarely went there, but it was always nice to know that when we did that we would be welcome.

Helen and Larry Anderson were the proprietors and, I might say, "watch dogs." It was easier to get through the "eye of the needle" than to get past the entrance. It had what I can only call "speakeasy qualities," as I have imagined them. Also, it had absolutely the best steaks anyone ever put into their mouths anywhere, anytime. People would always ask Larry where he bought his steaks, and he would never tell, but rumor had it that he was seen buying filets of beef at the local A&P store.

Housed in an over-sized log cabin, the Embassy was a big, barny, gloomy place; but in the winter, with a roaring fire, it suddenly became inviting—that is, if you avoided the ladies room. Helen kept its temperature below freezing. On second thought, there might never have been heat installed in that area.

Helen's was the one place in a dry town and county that served you, as a guest, whatever you liked in the way of refreshments.

One packed evening, Jacques Fath appeared as a guest of another party. Among the crowd was one lady who was in a Jacques Fath suit—and happy. And there was another lady who did not wear her Jacques Fath suit and who was very unhappy! She was hysterically furious, proclaiming to one and all that she had planned to wear a Jacques Fath suit and changed her mind at the last moment!

Live entertainment often consisted of a small band and some audience participation. I shall never forget the hushed stillness, and silent curiosity, as Jacques Fath appeared at the mike and gave a throaty rendition of Noel Coward's "Mad About the Boy!"

Most evenings we would all wait until the orchestra had left, and would sit, spellbound, while Larry Anderson played the piano and forthcoming would be the most wonderful improvisations on the ivories that you could ever imagine. I've heard of other "performances," but they may only be hearsay! It was a gala evening, mainly personal, because Henry had just given me his mother's diamond ring. No engagement had been announced, except a pledge to ourselves, and we liked it that way.

The Embassy was located in the woods out at Sedgefield, and it seemed like a trip to get out there. Eventually it closed. It was said that as she was about to die, Helen hired an ambulance and rode around the high rent district of Greensboro pointing out a nice person here, and a nice person there, and on occasion, pointing out one she would call a witch—that's a five letter word that rhymes with dog…!

THE THREE R's—R#1 As a hostess, I am certain that I am not perfect, but I do try. Occasionally, however, my patience has been taxed beyond perfection. Three occasions stand out in my mind.

One was when we had just completed our home to a point where I felt that we should entertain. And it was certainly "our time" to show some *signs of* reciprocity.

Almost always, after a concert or recital, someone would give a reception. Having cleared arrangements with the host couple (pick up at train station and get them back to the train on time) I proceeded. All I wanted to do was to serve coffee and dessert at 10:30 in the evening. By the time I checked with the likes and wants of the artists and hosts included, we served the following: milk, beer, sandwiches, scrambled eggs, and coffee with dessert.

I held up very well until the "Star" of the evening, while sitting in the middle of my new sofa newly upholstered in white silk and linen damask from Scalamandré, waxed eloquent in broken English. I passed the sandwiches to him, and lo, he popped one (whole) into his mouth and then, with two strokes, wiped his hand on the cushion of said piece of furniture. My jaw dropped. Henry looked pale and stricken. Eventually, they left, and Henry, gracious host that he is, slammed the door and said only one word: "PEASANTS"

R#2 An unnamed client came by for drinks, one evening, with our friend who was the intermediary between the client and us. The gentleman was a student at a nearby college, from a very well known family, and "rich as Croesus." But he did not want anyone to know he was creating something beautiful for the school. I could not discuss with him our project. I was not supposed to know who he was and his name was not a familiar one. Henry Z, sleuth that he was, figured out exactly who he was and which bank he owned. The project was completed and paid for. But back to the evening with our client in our home, Mr. Client came in, was duly impressed with the surroundings, and sat down in one of my fine antique chairs, the legs of which went in four different directions! Embarrassment reigned on my part and his part. Chair was duly repaired and is holding up well, but let me assure you that if it ever goes up for sale, I will reveal the ancestry of Mr. Client from a famous family!

We were serving drinks before dinner, for this was big business. There were four gentlemen in the textile business and, of course, I fixed something for them to nibble on. I duly passed the bowl of pickled shrimp around once and put it on the tea table in front of the sofa, with picks, and a plate of cheese and crackers. Young Yuppie seated there, proceeded to do away with the entire dish of pickled shrimp, one by one. I watched until the bottom of the bowl was cleared, almost clean. This well-fed guest is now a television star of some magnitude in New York!!!

———•·•———

NEW YORK—My first trip to New York was with a friend. She wanted to go up and see some shows, and she invited me to go along. In the past I had been taught to think of New York as Sin City—gangsters, etc. So I was a little frightened. Little did I know then that much of my future, and certainly many of my thoughts, would be concerned with that bit of geography. This visit was to the Roosevelt Hotel. So I heard Guy Lombardo, saw the city from the top of the Empire State Building, dined at the restaurant at Rockefeller Center, saw the Rockettes, and shopped and went to the theatre. A solidly booked season, we were lucky to get tickets to three winners: Death of A Salesman, Kiss Me Kate, and South Pacific. A perfect introduction to New York City.

———•·•———

NEW YORK—Trips to New York were sometimes fearful. Residents of the city, whom we visited, had little interest in activities that I felt were great learning opportunities. Riding the subway and attending foreign movies with subtitles was strange. Attending services in beautiful churches and going to museums was much more my style.

On one trip, however, an invitation to join a business friend for the evening was most rewarding, and for the first time I felt that I was in the real New York. Arrival at the friend's apartment exposed Henry and me to an extremely different setting. It was in one of the glorious apartment buildings located on the west side of Central Park! We progressed from one hospitable hostess to another before going to dinner. A lady artist, who painted beautiful horses and handsome riders, allowed us to view her fine paintings. We then went to dinner at the Café d'Artists, and I was charmed.

After dinner, we returned to the elegant apartment house and attended a musical soiree. We were two among just a few guests enjoying the performance of talented singers, appropriately performing from a grand stairway and inside balconies in a two-story room. I was thrilled. I was really in the New York of my imagination!

Returning to our friend's apartment for the last social glass of the evening, I admired something in a frame hanging on the wall. As I left, it became a gift. A lady's lovely fan! I still enjoy it and remember that joyous occasion!

Installation in New York City was always a challenge. Dealing with the union workers made things move more slowly than we liked. And I could not always have my way. Stopping work at 4:30 P.M. in the afternoon was not my way of getting the job done. Of course we brought help up with us and kept going. Working until ten-thirty or eleven o'clock at night did not please the security officers. In fact, they were most reluctant for me to go out with my own fur coat over my shoulders.

We were furnishing a small one-bedroom apartment, and it was my decision that they should have a sofa long enough for someone to sleep on if necessary. I planned for this to be the perfect installation in a limited amount of time.

Three boys were given a very specific plan of where everything was to be put. I gave them a half-a-day ahead of me to get everything properly placed. Imagine my surprise to arrive the next morning to see my ninety-inch sofa sitting in the lobby. Shock turned to horror when I learned that it would not fit in the elevator, there was no service elevator, and the stairs were too narrow and a turn was not possible. Very often we could place a piece of furniture on top of the carrier cabin and ride it almost to the top and lift it off. Not so this time. I was hysterical. My very competent husband simply suggested that I go away, promising that he would get the sofa upstairs.

"Go to Saks and spend the day, but not much money!" Henry said.

Not understanding the mechanics of big city installation, I was mystified! I went to Saks, but did not spend the day. By noon I was back at the apartment house. After all, this was St Patrick's Day and it would be very difficult to get help, especially on short notice. Arriving at the apartment, I was stunned to see traffic averted and my sofa going up the side of the building and in through the window. The usual "no problem" turned out to be just that!

"Virginia, how do you think all those baby grand pianos get into penthouse apartments?"

"No problem" was as follows: Henry immediately hired a glazier to remove the large picture window and stand by to close up the window. Then he immediately found a dealer in jacks for the roof to get the sofa up and into the apartment. The glazier got the window back in place by noon! I showed up and believed in miracles. Happily, the occupant liked everything. He had seen nothing until it was completely finished, down to the silver saccharin holder! That went up in the palm of my hand.

Sunday in New York after church at St. Bartholomew's and lunch, we planned to see a movie. As we stepped out into the street, we turned to see someone (a vagrant?) throwing a large trashcan into a store window. Of course, it shattered and he ran. The window was a display of one of the larger fabric houses that we patronized. Henry called the manager to let him know what had happened. The police arrived and we moved on. My thoughts? What a horrible place to live. Was every one so mean and careless?

We were walking to the little theatre near the Plaza Hotel. We stopped by the light at Park Avenue, and Henry became engaged in conversation with a very nice looking gentleman. He asked where we were from and we exchanged courtesies. His grandfather had been a diplomat at the court in St. Petersburg before you-know-what happened and he was now a citizen of this country. When he found out what movie we were going to see, he said the next show would be at 5 P.M. He suggested we go to the Plaza and have tea. He handed us tickets to the movie and told us to use them for admission. He was the manager of that theatre. My thoughts? What a nice thing to have happen. Not everyone was mean and someone had been very thoughtful to us strangers visiting the city.

I remember another pleasurable moment in New York. Henry had grown a beard. In 1958 our town was celebrating the 150th anniversary of its founding. In the spirit of the occasion, all male citizens were encouraged to grow beards, and Henry Zenke fell right in with the idea. His father had a beard, so why shouldn't he? He really was very handsome and the beard enhanced his handsomeness.

When in New York, he would always get his hair done by the barber in the basement of Radio City. That day, he walked in with a full beard, which was in need of trimming. And it was a great joy to that barber, for he was no ordinary barber—he had been a featured beard trimmer at the court of the last Czar. And such a job he did on Henry, and the beard made him very distinguished.

I waited for Henry to leave the barber and as he appeared, I fell in love all over again with this wonderful person with whom I was privileged to walk through life!

———•◦•———

I often feared trips to New York. We went, usually, to visit Henry's family, and later on to do work for the family business. Conversations with the family were often highly seasoned with peppery exchanges of personal opinions. I eventually came to dread these events. (But later on we would stay at the company apartment or at the apartment of clients—and I enjoyed these occasions.)

On one such visit to the family, Henry and I announced that we were planning a trip to Europe to visit Henry's wartime sites and the family he had lived with during the war. We thought that our plans would bring joy to everyone. By the end of that day, the wrath of all the Germans was on our heads for lack of some other simple explanation.

It was days later before I realized the real reason for the wrath. Henry was taking me to Europe before his revered sibling got to make the much longed-for trip back to the German "fatherland." But go we did and somehow survived.

A year or so later, Henry's sibling got to make the pilgrimage, and we were "off the hook," so to speak. It was not our original plan to be in attendance at the departure of his sister and family, but off to New York we went. Our daughter had arrived and was just beginning to toddle. She went with us but was left in the care of the housekeeper while we bade everyone bon voyage.

(Carrying luggage and attending to the transferal of life on land to life on sea, for traveling relatives was our real reason for going.) We remained at the house for a few days to clean up some matters, and one day I was actually left alone to play with my young daughter and read and just enjoy myself.

On this day, I was to be subjected to a most horrifying experience! The mailman arrived and I went to answer the ring. As I was standing in the doorway, a draft went through the house so forceful that the heavy storm door slammed against my back and pushed me outside. To my horror, the door locked behind me. My small daughter was crawling around inside, and the iron was hooked up, the cord plugged into an outlet at floor level!!! Needless to say, I panicked. As any Southern girl would do, I checked the neighbors on either side. No answer. To get to the back door, I had to go all the way around the block of row-houses. No way to get in. What could I do? It then dawned on me. I was a stranger in this strange town. It was a lovely neighborhood and I had never even been introduced to anyone in the area. Now, to a little girl from down South, this is like being in a foreign country. It was unthinkable that these people did not know their neighbors and in turn were not known by them. I was scared. Henry would not be back from the city until six o'clock and it was only lunch time. I began to run, hoping to find a human being who could help me. As I was going around the block to the back of the house, I noticed that there was a window open on the third floor, the only way in. Two or three houses away there were some painters working on a house and they had tall ladders. As

I tried to explain my predicament to them I began to cry. I promised all the money I had in my purse if one would only take the ladder, go in the upper window and let me in the door that had slammed locked. "Lady, I could go to jail for this," said the painter. I finally prevailed and one gentleman agreed. I had to go all the way around three sides of the block to get to the front door. Then I really did start to worry again. Suppose the man did not let me in. Suppose he harassed my child or worse, suppose he fell off the ladder and suppose, suppose… By that time, I was at the front door. The gentleman opened it for me and held it while I got in to find my daughter, safe. Thank God! But why thank God? It was the man on the ladder who helped me. But then, God comes in different forms. I emptied my wallet, which he declined, but I insisted. And I collapsed, daughter in arms, and did not let her go. I wanted to be home, not go home, but be home.

The only logical ending to this frightful episode was to get away. Several blocks away there was a lovely inn. I put precious child in the perambulator, took her down to the inn, and ordered whiskey sours and lobster salad. I sat where I could see Henry come out off the tube, and could pay the bill.

Henry suffered large doubts about my story, especially the part about talking the painter into "climbing and entering." After all, this was New York City, where neighbors might not know neighbors.

———•◦•———

NEW YORK SHOPPING—Shopping for antiques in New York can be fun—tiring, but fun—especially if you have money, good credit, and a willing and waiting client.

This day, we had all three. It was such a pleasure to see all the beautiful pieces of furniture and accessories, and to wonder where they all came from or who once owned them. The trap in these excursions occurs when you see something that you want but it is too expensive for you to purchase. On to the next dealer and the next one, etc. There you run into the same item, or something similar, that you cannot afford to purchase because it is even more expensive than the first piece you couldn't buy! Turn around, hurry back to the first shop, and purchase the piece you admired, because by now, it is a bargain! I fall into this trap every time I shop.

This day, we were shown many nice things and did purchase some. But the thing that consumed our interest was a room full of beautiful English pine paneling and mantelpieces, along with original hardware, crisp carving in a soft old finish, and from a house in England. It was the very thing we needed for an old house we were remaking in a nearby town. Alas, it was sold, and not available to us. Henry, who loved beautiful woods and architectural splendor, kept admiring it, and kept the conversation going. The dealers were a family we had done business with for many years. Apparently, that day, they were impressed with the money we were turning loose.

And so, the salesman said, "Let me check on something. It has been 'on hold' for this customer for some time."

Ah! so. The salesman returned to Henry and, after some toned-down conversation, really a whisper, admitted that they would consider a sale. Their client had not made any payment on the paneling, and it had been on hold for over a year!

Money changed hands and we picked it up and carried it back to North Carolina and created two beautiful rooms with it. Happy Henry. Happy clients! The unhappy loser of these beautiful goods was none other than the wife of the president of a country in the far Pacific. She had wanted to purchase the pieces before she and all her shoes got dethroned.

HOSPITALITY—Sometimes I think, I guess I know, that hospitality is like a ghost. It is a presence more than lemonade, iced tea, and fried chicken on Sunday. It is something you feel or sense.

Once, we were driving home from New York. It seemed only proper for us to stop by to see relatives. It was getting late but we did so anyway. I guess we were hoping to be invited to spend the night. Relations had been strained for some time but we kept hoping they would improve. We had just had such a happy trip to the big city. Our beautiful daughter had been presented at a ball in New York City. Her father was so proud. It was his hometown. Later analysis made him unclear how it all happened. As our daughter summed it up, "He just doesn't understand Southern blood lines."

Our detailed description of fun in New York fell on deaf ears with the relatives. It was a cold January night outside, but even colder inside.

We got up to leave and were presented with the thought that we could spend tonight "at the other house, if we wanted to!!!" My deepest feeling was that we would be much better off and more welcome at some strange motel along the highway. I was right!!!

Stopping for lunch the next day in Bowling Green, I realized that we were very close to a plantation that I wanted to see. It was on the south side of the Rappahannock—we were near it. As we got into the car, I suggested that we drive to it just to see the house and setting. Henry agreed and we took the drive to the front door of the house. A bitter cold but sunny January day, I only wanted to let the owners know that we were architectural historians and very much interested in the structure. And I started to the front door.

Henry said, "Oh, that's not necessary."

But I was more comfortable doing what I thought was polite. At the door, I was greeted by a gentleman in country, but elegant, tweeds. I introduced myself and explained by mission.

"Child, come in here out of the cold."

"Oh no! We only wanted to walk around the grounds."

Behind him appeared the lady of the house in a country, but elegant, Davidow Suit.

"Come in, my child, out of the cold."

With that I had to explain that my family was in the car and we were on our way home.

"Bring them in, by all means. Come in by the fire and get warm."

With that, we were welcomed by Mr. and Mrs. Pratt, the owners, who graciously received us and gave us a guided tour of their home, with its original furnishings of the period. We must have been there over an hour and were made so comfortable. I could only think to myself, here we are, being entertained by such genteel hosts who had never laid eyes on us. What a memory for the four Zenkes, particularly after the unfortunate reception of the night before.

One never knows when graciousness and hospitality will be extended. Once while traveling to a nearby town, we had a minor car accident, not our fault, but it was, nonetheless, an unfortunate thing to have happen.

We could still drive, so eventually we went on our way. But while we were waiting for the state troopers, I just sat in the car by the side of the road.

Very soon, a young lady, with a baby in her arms, came out of a roadside mobile home nearby and offered help. "You would be much better off waiting in my home. Let me give you something to drink. Tea maybe?"

I was overwhelmed by her consideration and thoughtfulness. Such graciousness found at an unexpected place during an inconvenient time. I shall never forget. And each time I take that road north, I pause and reflect on my aunt, who once said, "You never know where you will find character and genius."

Another occasion of unexpected hospitality took place in North Georgia in 1931 at the plantation of my great great grandparents. I was about seven or eight years old and my mother, father, sister, and I were visiting my mother's family in Gwinnett County. Back in 1931, there were still a lot of roads that were unpaved, main roads, and it had been an arduous trip.

I wanted very much to see the old "plantation home," nothing too fancy but still interesting. A frame house with porches in all the right places and the most gorgeous English Boxwood bushes all around. The family cemetery was across the road, twin cedars towering over the gravesites of twin daughters lost many years ago. The remains of a revolutionary ancestor and others, with fieldstones marking the gravesites of family servants.

Nothing was spared to help me share in past history, but the real event of the day was when we stopped to visit "Green and Edie," still living near the old house. We had lunch (dinner in the middle of the day) in a very neat and clean cottage, and many tales of my ancestors were told. "Green and Edie" were pleased to see Miss Cora's family. And I was in awe of it all, for, you see, "Green" had been born a slave, before the late unpleasantness. Edie had always been free, but not Green. He had belonged to my family.

Somehow, after that, I felt that I had been back in time, and with no sense of remorse or regret, just a joyous few hours for us all.

———⋅•⋅———

VISITING—Visiting has never been my strong suit, especially over night. When dark comes, I want to be home. Likewise, I do not like to entertain overnight guests. I am not at all like my mother, who wanted to entertain everybody, for any length of time.

Once, however, we did accept an invitation to visit with some friends in South Carolina. We had met them at Hilton Head and found them most enjoyable. They owned vast acreage in the foothills and were very productive, agriculturally, and definitely lived the good life—traveled a lot and were descended from notables in the history of that state. So we went for a visit. Driving down from Columbia, settlements and towns became scarce and we found ourselves driving around without being sure that we were on the right road.

"Why don't we stop and ask somebody for directions?" I suggested.

That was silly. There was no one in sight, besides which, nothing and no one could ever get Henry to stop and ask for help. He would just keep driving. The only humans we saw on that lonely country road turned out to be a state patrolman giving a ticket to someone. Henry finally got his nerve up and stopped to speak to the officer—and asked if he knew where our host might live.

The officer snapped to attention with a healthy salute, handed the driver's license back to the offender, and said, "Yes, sir, follow me."

Henry was overwhelmed at this local southern efficiency, and shortly we arrived, with escort, where the lord of the manor lived.

The feudal system was still very much intact in some sections of rural South Carolina.

—•◆•—

BELMEAD—Leaving Richmond one afternoon after lunch, I suggested that we take time to locate Belmead, the Philip St. George Cocke home on the south side of the James River, west of Richmond.

Unknown territory to us, we found it without too much trouble. We crossed a deep creek—almost forded it—and went up a steep hill to view a spectacular situation. The house seemed enormous and I felt as if we were somewhere in middle Europe. The house was designed by A.J. Davis, the same architect who designed our Blandwood, Governor John Motley

Morehead's home, in Greensboro, and was a great example of what not to expect of a Virginia plantation.

At this point in time, it was used as a Catholic military school for black men and boys. We were welcomed by silence, total silence, and no sight of any one. Eventually, a priest in khakis approached us and spoke. He was blond, thirty-ish, and had the "map of Ireland" all over his face—to quote Henry, with a brogue to match. We explained our interest in the house because of A. J. Davis, the architect, and he quickly answered, "Yes, I know about Jefferson Davis."

Henry and I dropped the subject. The priest explained that he could not take us through the house because it was homecoming weekend.

Still total silence—no noise at all.

We were allowed to walk around the house and stand on the terraces to behold a beautiful view of a turn in the James River—very close to overflowing at that time. It was the very spot where Philip St George Cocke took his life when he learned that, possibly instead of himself, Robert E. Lee had been made head of the confederate forces. It was a beautiful spot, especially the carriage house, which was located underground. But we needed to move on and finish our journey. We made our manners to the Irish priest and started to the car.

There was one rose blooming, definitely the "last rose of summer." And, as we passed, the priest picked the beautiful pink rose and handed it gently to me!

Henry smiled and we both wondered about the loneliness of this spot that served to isolate him from the rest of the world. It is now a pressed rose in some volume of *Virginia Architecture* in my library.

——•◆•——

PLANTATION!—Why does that word intrigue me so? It has all my life, even before Hollywood caught on to its possibilities. The dictionary says: "a cluster of plantings all in one spot." For me, it always conjures up the most historic and romantic thoughts, good and bad.

My earliest memories are of being with my grandparents. Their land was not a large holding, but it had a wonderful old house that I wish had not burned in 1941. How depressed I felt. What, to them was not important then, there was no electricity, and my first Christmas there was no Christmas at all without lights on the tree.

We made up for that lack with firecrackers and fireworks with "sparklers," one of which ignited my new cotton flannel bathrobe and I was aflame, alone on the front porch. Of course, I screamed and thankfully had presence of mind enough to start rolling on the floor. Stopped the flames but ruined my new Christmas present.

Middleton and Magnolia Plantations on the Ashley River were among my earliest passions. They were not glorified, as they are now, but very much there. It was so romantic to think of the owners going out to Middleton for the summer one year and never going back to their home in the city, but staying there to recreate that beautiful spot. And Magnolia I always loved and enjoyed.

Years later, Alonzo Hall, a college professor of English, whom I adored, explained that if beauty is in the eye of the beholder, so is possession of what you see. At that moment of beholding, there is no one else to receive and accept the vision except you. Then you are its sole possessor at that time! "If the tree falls and there is no one there to hear it, did it make a noise?"

Once back in 1937, in Virginia, we were planning to visit Charleston. A young navy man at the base in Norfolk wanted to go home to Charleston for Thanksgiving and, as we were driving down, we offered to take him home. Home to him was Mulberry plantation on the Cooper River.

The trip was a long one and we arrived at about one o'clock in the morning. I was thrilled. I had always wondered what was behind those brick pillared gates, and now I would find out. There were miles and miles of dirt road under Gothic-like ceilings of Spanish moss. Too sleepy to notice anything else, I fell asleep in the guesthouse at Mulberry. Our hosts, the family of our traveling companion, made us most welcome and bedded us down for the night, showering us with hospitality. They were the resident managers of the plantation.

The next morning before anyone else was up I stepped out to survey the site. Such a morning, I will never forget. In the fall, the sun just coming up over the misty Cooper River, early camellias were in bloom and I was alone, walking through the garden around the old house. It was so special. There was no one else to behold it and I absorbed the vision in its entirety. So, according to my English professor, for the moment I owned it.

I went back to the guesthouse, and had a breakfast of codfish and grits. I'd never tasted codfish before then, or since, but a scented memory remains.

———•◦•———

MORE PLANTATIONS—Being from the tidewater, I always felt that I would never get to see a plantation called Berry Hill. At least not the one described in history books as being so remote. Every county has a Berry Hill. When I woke up one day and realized that Berry Hill neighbored me in Halifax County in Virginia, I was beside myself with joy. Our Tarover had been the original home of the Bruces in that part of Virginia and had been built by the son of Berry Hill's owner. Staunton Hill in Charlotte County was built by a Charles Bruce, a half-brother, and all three houses were designed or influenced by John Evans Johnson. So we felt a kinship to both of these structures.

We got to see and enjoy the hospitality of Berry Hill when its then owner and his daughter shared it with us. As it was, getting to see Staunton Hill was a bit more difficult. I finally got up the nerve and called the owner, Ambassador David K.E. Bruce. And gracious he was, indeed, and he granted us permission to see the grounds, informing his manager that we would arrive.

The approach to the house was through what seemed like miles of forests, winding around until we arrived at the house. It was a pure neo-Gothic structure, a form I had never admired, but could only be impressed by the thoroughness and completeness of the whole development. This was a plantation that had survived *the War*, and was still productive when others had failed—so remote, then and now. Later, the son, David Bruce, visited us at Tarover and we were to enjoy visiting him at Staunton Hill. The house had been somewhat Georgianized, but was still impressive.

Later there was so much destruction of forests there, the approach is now devastating. Upon entering the gates, you can soon see the house, and what used to seem like miles away, is now only a short distance.

In the same area as these two plantations is one named Prestwould, in Mecklenburg County. Our first visit there was like a trip to England. The approach to the house was through straight lanes of enormous cedar trees bound by dry stone walls. It is such a shame that someone cut the trees away. The approach is not the same. But the house is now a happy historic spot where many can enjoy the house grounds and gracious garden parties, guided by a most capable director and staff.

VIRGINIA PLANTATION—Once, when traveling from east to west in Virginia, my parents and I stopped at several of the James River plantations. All memorable, one stands out.

The owner, at that time a bachelor, and descendant of the builder, was absent and his housekeeper did the honors. In the nicest and most possible way, I regarded her as the consummate "mammy." She graciously showed us around and kept giving me what I thought was the evil eye. What was I doing traveling alone with my parents? She finally asked if I was married. To which I replied, "Yes. I am to meet my husband in Lynchburg." We continued our tour of the house and as we were leaving, she turned and asked, "Are you sure you are married?" What did I miss?

WILTON—Crossing the bridge over the Piancatank River in Virginia, one does not see the precious small house known as Wilton. Only when we turned around and headed back to Yorktown did we see this charming house. It was an early eighteenth century brick structure with the addition at the back added later forming a T.

All efforts to penetrate the place and see the inside met with failure. We had been told that the paneled rooms were most exceptional; and, of course, we could figure out the plan of the rooms from the location of windows and chimneys.

Each visit was met with the same sense of frustration. If we saw anyone, including the owner, we were always told that they could not let anyone in because they had much restoration going on and did not want to let anyone in the house.

To all appearances, nothing had been done since the last time we were there or the time before that. On our last visit, the owner appeared as usual and I again made my plea. Only this time, I pushed the thought that we would most likely not come that way again. Apparently, he sensed the situation and realized that Henry would not be able to travel much more and conceded to let us into the interior.

It was all as I expected, the layout of rooms, the paneling and the location of the stairway; and, of course, a disappointment as to the upkeep. It was terribly neglected, but we did get to see it. Hopefully it is now in the hands of someone who cares for it, as we would have done.

A very recent "plantation trip" was to Romancoke, on a smaller river that joins the York River at West Point in Virginia, a social visit to the home that had been the residence of one of Robert E. Lee's sons. The owners were so gracious to share it and to be so hospitable after the burial of a close friend. It was in immaculate condition and obviously much loved. A joy to behold!

—∙+∙—

FIRST CAR—It was 1965. The long awaited arrival of Henry Christian Zenke, III brought changes to our life styles, all of which were hoped for and expected. But there was one major change in my life that had to take place, and it loomed larger than anything I had ever coped with. I had to learn to drive an automobile! At age forty-one, I could not drive a car! The chief reason was laziness. It was nice to be driven everywhere I needed to go. Next reason was that I did not own a vehicle of my very own. All cars in the family were company owned, and if you think I would have touched one of them, you are much misguided! But, with a daughter ready to attend school, something had to give, and it was a wife named Virginia.

At the end of the summer, sales were in evidence at all the dealerships and in the newspapers. I thoughtfully suggested to Henry that we look for a bargain for my first car. A kind smirk was the result.

"You learn to drive, and I will get you a car."

In those days, Greensboro was still a city with a downtown, and all the dealerships were within walking distance. On the days I had help with the children, I would get out and call upon the various showrooms. I wanted to be practical, so I started with a friend, who happened to be a dealer, but he had nothing at the "low end of the line" that would have been suitable. I went to Ford, Chevrolet, Pontiac, and to Oldsmobile, searching. At each encounter, the price kept going up! So back to Ford I went! The big problem was to get a salesman anywhere to pay attention to a lady who was considering the purchase of a car, especially if one of the children was accompanying me.

On my second visit to Ford, an item caught my eye and would not let go! It was squared–off in the front and back—a small two-door with no excessive hardware. It was neat-looking, and at the high end of the line. It was a Thunderbird! Rationalization set in, the same version I always used. That is, if I have to pay X number of dollars for something I barely like, why not add a few dollars more and get what I really want? This has always worked for me. When I buy something that is less expensive, just to get by, I end up buying something else to make it look better. Therefore, I am really saving money by buying the more expensive item in the first place. Right? Right!

I dutifully went through the agony of "guilt by extravagance" and finally arrived at the solution. I would invest in the Thunderbird.

I returned to the Ford showroom, this time with babe in arms. I waited for some attention. None was forthcoming. Eventually, I timidly asked if I could speak to the sales manager and eventually he appeared.

"So, do you have any other models of Thunderbirds available?"

"Let me take you out to the lot and show you what we have."

"That won't be necessary," I said. "If you have a list, just read it off to me."

Pause. The list was produced and there it was, dark gray, matching interior, automatic transmission and air-conditioned. I wanted it right that minute! I asked the price.

"I'll take it." At long last, I was invited into his office. Serious consideration was being given to how I could take care of my payments—and so:

"How would you like to handle this transaction?" was forthcoming.

Very simply, I replied, "I would like to pay cash."

At long last, I was invited to have a seat. I have never seen a spelling of the "clearing of the throat" in word form, so a lengthy pause will have to suffice. Lengthy pause.

"That is if you will accept a personal check and accommodate me on one condition?"

"What is that?" he asked.

"Sir, I need to have you store the car for a while."

"What do you mean?"

"Well, I do not know how to drive and must make some arrangements about learning and getting a license before I can take it away."

Lengthy pause again.

"And you plan to pay for it now?"

"Yes," I replied.

"When?"

"I said, now!"

The check was produced and signed, and he agreed to store the car for thirty or sixty days, hoping fervently that someone of my mentality could get through the test for a driver's license.

No conversation about this affair had transpired between anyone and me. I finally got the courage to look in the yellow pages and found an individual listed as a driving instructor. I made the appointment for once a week on the day I had help with the children. At 10:30 every Wednesday morning, this nice, toothless man came by in what could only be described as an out-of-date taxi and took me for a spin! Very exciting! We spent most of our hour tooling around the enormous parking lot of the War Memorial Coliseum (where there was nothing for me to hit). Meanwhile, the Thunderbird was in storage.

One hot fall afternoon, Henry came home for lunch and was in a black mood. He *had* to go out of town and there was not a vehicle on the place. His car was in the shop, company station wagon was in use, company "big car" was out of town, and not even a truck was available. He would have to call and cancel his important appointment! During lunch I pondered his problems, and my dilemma. This crisis just might be the answer to a prayer!

A bit fearful of my recent actions, I felt that Henry's predicament might prove the best solution for the process of revelation! Carefully timing the circumstances, I pulled a set of car keys from the pocket over my heart and said, "Please be my guest. If you will go down to the Ford place and buy a license plate and take out insurance, you may drive *my* car."

Silence—no, more than that—stony silence.

Henry went and picked up the car, but he suffered intense embarrassment when the insurance agent demanded to know how I planned to pay for the car. It was most painful for him to reply, "She paid cash."

Shortly thereafter, I did pass the driver's test and acquired the license. This new-found mobility enabled me to accomplish more work for loyal clients, and be more thoughtful to my friends. The day would eventually come when I would buy my own truck to deliver someone else's merchandise. Almost everyone was pleased that I could now "get around."

Only one negative comment came from my extended family, in a snooty tone of voice. "You didn't buy a car, you bought a Thunderbird."

My own expression of style, maybe?

———•·•———

WOODLANDS—Finally learning to drive and having my own automobile gave me a freedom to move around that I had not known. It also gave me no excuses for not going home to visit my widowed mother. These trips were about five hours long and I would occasionally get off the beaten path to avoid the dullness of the trip.

One day I was traveling alone, and I approached a crossing and wondered what might be down the road going toward the Roanoke River. I wondered and I wandered. Back roads always have appealed to me more than the major highways. And this day, I really enjoyed the one on which I was traveling.

It was a summer day and the green forests of Virginia were beautiful as usual. I suddenly passed an entrance to what I can only describe as a vacant place, to me a secret garden. I was so surprised to find this old plantation on this route. A small sign proclaimed the name and date—an old brick house that predated the columns that had been added. There was no one in sight and I just enjoyed the place and the moment, feeling that I was at a secret historic spot, and I eventually continued on to Mother's.

Some months later, I met the owner of Woodlands and enjoyed her friendship as well as her home. It was a Roanoke River plantation on the Virginia side, but enjoyed connections with the families of Carolina across the river, especially the horsey set. We were invited to several parties and took pleasure in many visits with the owner.

And such history was stacked in that house. To stand in the central hall and behold something like eight antique corner cupboards was just the beginning. A portrait over the dining room mantelpiece provoked inquiry on my part. The reply: "Oh, you wouldn't know about him." Oh yes I would. He was the minister who married Peggy O'Neal and John Eaton, otherwise known as Joan Crawford and Franchot Tone in *The Gorgeous Hussy*. Every item in the house seemed to be of historic significance.

Arriving one afternoon for a visit, we were invited to come to the kitchen for a drink. Silver tumblers were fetched, tarnished—black silver tumblers. They had not felt the back of chamois cloth in years. But no matter about that, hospitality was abundant.

My answer to the invitation to have a drink in the kitchen was simply, "No, not when we can sit under the columns on the front porch."

And that we did.

These trips alone always provided many telephone calls between Henry and my mother. Henry would call when I left, to let Mother know that I would arrive about five hours later. Five hours later, Mother would call to tell Henry that I had not arrived and "something must have happened to me!" What? Two or three hours later provided more telephone calls and much conversation.

Finally safe arrival produced only chagrin. Was I "never to be trusted?"

And that particular trip on that day, while it was fun for me, I did realize that I was traveling a lonely road in a lonely area of the state. Something could have happened and I realized what worry I was causing.

Another time, I made that tedious trip, drove straight home to arrive at the tunnel under the Elizabeth River with no money. No cash any way. There I was in my new car, fine winter clothes, and fur hat to please my mother, and no loose change! Back up, get back to the highway and drive almost to the nearby state line in order to cross the river and get home for free!

HIGH SCHOOL—In high school we occasionally had substitute teachers—
and one day we all went to class, and sure enough a substitute was sitting
behind the desk. I think it was an English class, but we certainly got off on
a different subject very quickly. Our whole town, or city, was awash with
British sailors of the king's navy. It was all supposed to be very hush-hush
and an unknown fact, but an English aircraft carrier had limped into our
port for repairs! We were all very close to the war situation, somehow our
substitute teacher got off on the subject of World War I (we were sitting
through World War II)—and how it got started.

She gave us a fascinating version of the situation in Europe in 1914. The
colorful story of the romance of Franz Joseph of Austria and how he fell
in love with Elizabeth, the younger sister of the girl he was engaged to. I
was enthralled.

"And furthermore," she said, "We could see it all in the movies—with
Franchet Tone and Grace Moone."

I couldn't believe it. *The King Steps Out* was the same story she told us
about and I believed every word she said, with "stars in my eyes."

The story she told led me into an everlasting study of the Austrian-
Hungarian empire. And to this day, if I do not hear or read something
periodically about the history of middle Europe, I feel deprived.
Someday—someday I just thought to myself, I will go to Vienna, I will be
with all these people I have read about. Someday I will go there and waltz
and waltz and waltz—just like in the movies—someday I will.

Someday I did–just like in the movies.

Among my classmates that day was Herb Jones. He sat at the desk in
front of me and would often turn around to talk to me. Herb liked to paint,
so I spent time encouraging the process. He also suffered from migraine
headaches and missed a lot of school days. One day we got caught talking
in class and had to stay after school for a lecture. Herb and I sang in the
same church choir and could render some great duets, especially "Joy to
the World" at Christmas time.

Visiting Mother always meant a round of visits to and from friends of hers. So many of my friends lived elsewhere and we had lost touch.

One day she did ask me, "Is there anything you would like to do today?"

Thoughtfully, I replied, "Yes, I would like to visit with Herb Jones." He and his wife lived all of four blocks away. So it was not too troublesome.

"What in the world do you want to visit him for?"

I persisted and we did call on the Jones family. Mother and I arrived at the Jones house. Herb had converted the garage part of their home to a studio and was painting for a living. Mother and his wife went into the living room for a long visit and Herb and I enjoyed all his paintings. He specialized in boats and seascapes, and had done a number of shows and was doing well selling his work to offices, banks, and public institutions. He had also bought into a printing business and sold signed prints of his work; and then he decided to go into the framing business. He would buy old barns and such to get distressed wood and do his own framing. He had it made! The money was rolling in, and they still lived in the simple surroundings of his childhood. He would not make public appearances unless he was forced to; still the same Herb.

I finally admitted that I would like to own one of his paintings. He chuckled. "Virginia, you couldn't even afford to *talk* about owning one, they are expensive, selling for thousands of dollars apiece."

I chuckled. At home I still had two of his creations on clean shirt cardboards, done while he was in high school, crude but signed.

Our visit ended and as Mother and I left, she asked if I had enjoyed the visit.

I said, "Yes."

And she said, "That's interesting. Herb is nice, but it's too bad he never amounted to very much!!!"

There was no reply on my part. Logic could only make me realize that if Herb had not "amounted to very much" in her eyes then neither had I "amounted to very much."

———··◆··———

CHRISTMAS TOYS—Christmas is always more fun when the children are small and the level of expectancy is very high.

One year, the year of the "Hot Wheels" product, was to be memorable.

My mother was to arrive to be with us for the occasion, so plans were extensive. She would always arrive and ask, "When are you and Henry going to build a nice home for yourselves?"

Thud! One friend of ours always laughed at this and remarked, "She doesn't know that you and Henry are not camping out, does she?"

No matter how beautiful the house was it was not in the right section of town! Location, location, location.

Our son Chris had arrived and was an added joy. Christmas morning came and Santa Claus had arrived to leave an enormous number of presents. Among them, Hot Wheels and more Hot Wheels, a set from Grandmother, a set from God mother, and a set from far away. Little orange plastic tracks ran all over the house, up and down, and to my concern, they did not match anything in the house!

Christmas night, Henry and I were invited out to supper at a friend's annual party and Mother was elected babysitter. We returned to find Mother enjoying her grandchildren, but with a bit of concern about them. In the middle of the living room, cleared of orange plastic cars, there was a rather large creation of what appeared to be an airplane, constructed entirely of the pretty throw pillows gathered from throughout the house. The body of the plane was made of long rectangular pillows, the wings of plane of long narrow pillows, the wheels of round pillows, the steering gear of smaller round pillows, and the tail of the plane was of even smaller pillows, like the ones used for the propeller.

And Grandmother, standing off to the side, announced, in a clear voice, "I will never go out and spend money on toys for these children again. With their imaginations, who needs toys?"

She should not have been surprised. She must have forgotten how much fun I had with the contents of her button box, providing elegant wedding parties, classrooms, and picnics.

Having a sister who is very talented, more talented than I, sometimes made me uncomfortable, but not often. I was really very proud of her in spite of the fact that she diligently destroyed most of my beautiful toys. It served me right. Before she was born, I carefully prayed each night that God would not send me a brother, because boys are so destructive! Be careful what you pray for.

Each day when I returned from school, I was met at the door with, "'Suster,' I'm sorry."

And I would find another toy altered from its original.

Of course she got over this and was a beautiful young lady, with lovely blond braids that fell to her waist. And she became a very talented artist with a beautiful, professionally trained, soprano voice! She was soloist in the church choir and runner-up one year for the "Miss Norfolk" title.

One day, while practicing at church, her tunes switched to more secular themes. The organist pushed the wrong button while rehearsing, and "Ah Sweet Mystery of Life" by Victor Herbert swelled to enormous proportions, as it rolled from the church spire, to the shock of the surrounding community.

I'm not certain if this episode has been lived down to this day!

——•◆•——

1964—It was a Saturday morning in early spring. I was up and dressed and ready to enjoy a day at home. The house was clean and food had been prepared for the weekend. So there was a measure of contentment.

The phone rang and Henry said, "What are you doing?"

I have learned through the years that the translation of that interrogation phrase is usually something else, like, "Can you fix an extra plate for dinner?" This time it was different, quite different. I was informed that the editor of *House Beautiful* was at the office and wanted to come over to see what we had done to our house.

I was in shock and suggested that there was no reason for this and said, "maybe later in the day."

By this time, there was a slight knock at the door. A party of four had arrived and was perusing all the facets of my home. Frances Heard was the editor and a very clever, intuitive person.

She walked around and authoritatively said, "This is good. We can do a full-page on this. Hard to get a good angle on this, but we will manage."

About this time, Virginia surfaced mentally and said, "This *is* my home.

I have not said that anyone could do anything."

Toes were being stepped on and they were mine. Henry on one side and big boss on the other, and I felt the crunch!

Now, Frances Heard was a smart lady. I emphasize lady. A southerner with very good manners, who should have been in the diplomatic corps at the State Department. She sized me up immediately and from then on favored my home and me, and ultimately had her way about everything.

After a short visit, the dignitaries departed with the promise that they would return to photograph a couple of months later. That, I thought, was the end of that! I had known of so many photographs taken and never published that I dismissed it all from my mind. After all, who would want their privacy invaded and spread all over the country?

A few months later, they arrived. "They" being the editor, Frances Heard, her assistant, the very good photographer, Philip Roedel, and his assistant. They quietly invaded my home and set-up for a photography session. It lasted for four days. They came early and stayed late. They were fed lunch and supper and continued to work. Pluses: They did not smoke and were all very easy to get along with and be around; they graciously accepted any food I prepared; and I actually enjoyed them all. Again, Frances was very astute. She let me arrange my own flowers and place them where I wanted them. After each set-up, she turned and said, "Now, Virginia, you take a look at this and see what you think." And, of course, everything was upside down in the camera. Happily, I had studied photography for two years in college and was not necessarily out in left field. The sessions continued. I had worked very hard to have everything just right. They went around putting long pins in puffs and creases to hold everything in place. Years later, I would still find a three inch pin holding something together.

I had polished to perfection all of our silver and brass, only to have them go around and spray everything to make it dull, better for viewing by the camera. I soon learned that many accessories and books were placed askew to photograph at a better angle.

This being a family affair, our young, precious daughter would go around and straighten everything. "Mother has it this way," she would say, all this to the chagrin of the photographer. So she was farmed out for the next two days so we could get finished.

And they departed at last, leaving us with a very nice feeling about those talented people who worked so well together!

And so we put it out of our minds. I repeat, "There had been so many houses photographed and the results were never published or they were filed and forgotten. So be it."

Frances discussed with Henry and me the possibility of using all this information, with our house on the front cover of an issue, as a feature

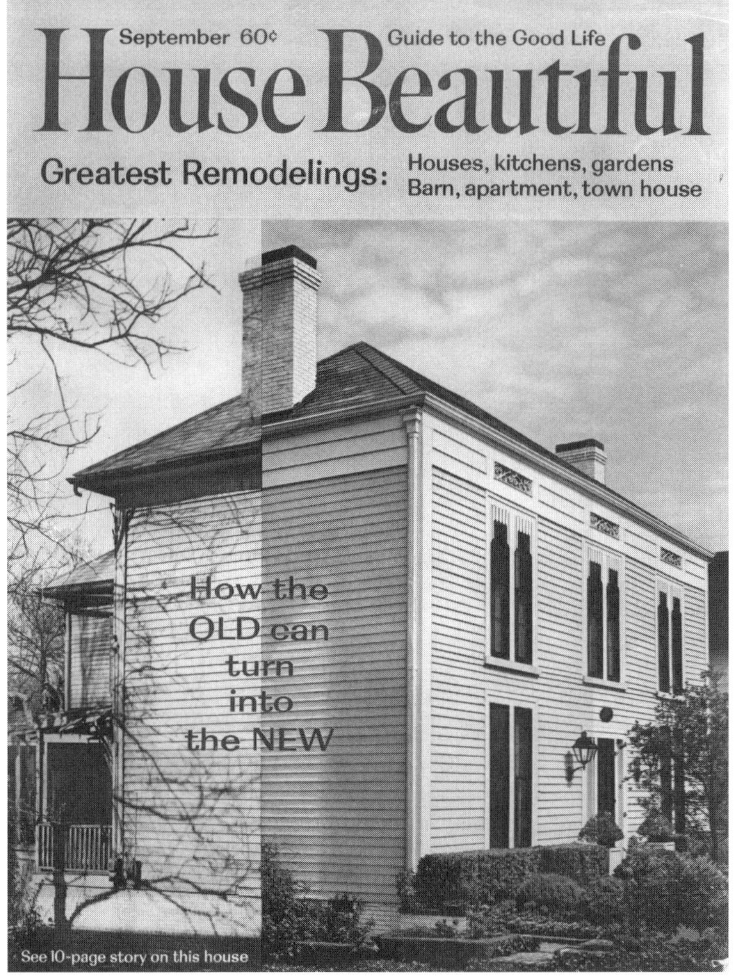

article. We were flattered, of course, and heartily agreed with the idea of a divided photograph on the front, a before and after composition. This would tell the story immediately. Before and after.

A concentrated effort was made by boss man to bump the cover idea and use instead a picture of a pretty inside room.

Frances stuck with me in what I considered important. All this effort did come out in the September issue, which was record timing. The front cover did it. Within two weeks time, all issues were sold out and people who tried to get a copy at the stands thereafter did not. Eventually two copies were found in Bermuda and a few in Oregon State. They were real collectors items. Now, happily, a few copies are being returned to me as people clean out their bookcases and attics.

And the fan mail! What a joy to receive letters from people all over the country and how our home related to their thoughts. All praises. And, on the Sunday after publication, we reveled in the cars passing by full with people staring at the house. It was a very "September in the Rain" occasion. And we thought, as they passed by, wouldn't all those people be touched by the fact that we were having breakfast by the fire with hot chocolate, Sunday newspapers scattered all over the floor, providing a very lived-in appearance for what looked so perfect in the magazine? Thank you, Frances Heard and *House Beautiful*.

—•◦•—

MOVIES—What was it about Hollywood that made it so important in my life, and maybe yours? As I look back on those motion pictures of the 30s and early 40s, I realize that I was not only being entertained, but very much informed, for I learned so much from the sets and costumes that would influence me in my work. Not just that either. So much history was really genuinely interpreted. Seldom did they stray far from the actual events. Only once was I offended when someone from Savannah, of 1790, was going to a party in Atlanta!!!! Not even a crossroads at that time! So be it. It was a pleasure to watch and enjoy all those films.

Being in my teens, I would fall in love periodically with the leading men, and they changed from time to time, until one day, Nelson Eddy appeared on the screen and that was it! No matter that he was in love with Jeannette MacDonald, or should be. I adored him. His presence, his manner, and the "way he handled her," to quote one of my Sunday school teachers, "Oh my!"

And the day I watched Jeanette in the swinging episode in *Maytime*. How? I know not. But just twenty seconds on the screen and I was a different person.

Years later, we were in France, and Henry took me to the Porcelain Museum at Sevres, and there I was staring at the same background that was used in the movie, (*Maytime*) St. Cloud on May Day. Henry did not know that was where we were and I said nothing, just enjoyed the moment. Besides, he would not sing "Will You Remember??

The year before Nelson Eddy died, he came to our town to perform with Guy Lombardo for Christmas. I bought the front row of seats that turned into a command performance for me and my friends.

A friend of ours, "Rosie," had become acquainted with Nelson Eddy, and each year at Christmas, she sent him a Virginia ham.

So when he was to visit Greensboro to perform, we thought it would be nice to entertain him after the concert. He was not registered at any hotel. So "Rosie" went to the local grade school and picked up my young daughter, simply saying, to her second grade teacher, that she wanted to take Ginia to find Nelson Eddy! Can you imagine that? Today it would be considered kidnapping! But find him "Rosie" did. And our young daughter was very surprised to discover that "he is old, Mother! Did you know that?"

I shall, however, always remember his diplomacy when, in the presence of several mature, well-dressed ladies, he patted my daughter on the head and said, "Ah, Ginia, the fairest of them all."

We went backstage and nothing could prevail upon him to come by for coffee, friendship, and Virginia ham and eggs with a glass of Tokay wine. His troupe had to perform elsewhere the next day. He looked so tired.

But there he was, still handsome in his navy blue cashmere coat and gray Fedora, and white scarf at his throat. It was good to meet him in person. He was so gracious and smiled at all of us ladies (all dressed up for the occasion).

As he turned to leave, he picked up a heavy suitcase.

Gut reaction took place and my arm flew out and hit Henry in the middle! "You are *not* going to let that man carry his own valise, are you?"

"I am," he replied.

Within six months Nelson Eddy was dead.

If you think that's the end, you are wrong. Chris and I were driving to New York. Our first run to the big city with just the two of us and, as usual, I made a joyride out of the trip whenever possible. One night, we were on Kent Island and we ate delicious crab cakes! The next morning, we were up and off to Philadelphia, where I remembered antiques shops with so many good buys. We checked into the Four Seasons Hotel and it was almost time for the shops to close, but I suggested that we window-shop anyway. Six o'clock came and every place was closed.

We had walked so far that I did not feel like walking all the way back to the hotel. The one-way streets provided a taxi going south when we were supposed to be going north. I suddenly realized that this was my son's first visit to the city and asked the driver to, if he had time, please run us by the Liberty Bell and Independence Hall. He did so gladly. "No problem."

Eventually we turned back north and I finally thought to ask him if he knew how to get to the Church of Our Savior, the Episcopal Cathedral Church of Philadelphia. He said, "Yes."

I then said, "How far?"

He said, "Thirty blocks or so."

I then said, "Will you please drive us there?" He did so, not necessarily gladly, and definitely left out, "No problem."

One-way streets again took us around the cathedral. The front door was open (painted red) on a very dark stone church. The taxi driver parked around the corner, and I admonished him and Chris to stay right there until I took a quick look inside the church. Nothing strange about that. I go into churches anywhere and everywhere, all over the world. By the time I got to the front door, it was closed, locked! Evensong was over. Not to be outdone at this point, I headed for the entrance to the offices of the church. And there, before me, stood what must have been the rector, himself. And there was Virginia herself with head covering and short white gloves appealingly asking, "Is the church closed?"

"Well, just about, the lights are off. What can I do for you, my child?"

Sixty if I was a day. "Oh, sir, I have always wanted to visit this sanctuary."

"Well, my child, I will let you visit it. Come along!"

"Oh, but sir, I hate to take your time. First let me ask. Did you ever have a member of your choir who was handsome, blond, and became a famous concert singer?"

With an enormous grin, "Do come along, my child."

It was such a joy to be in the church and allowed to sit in exactly the same spot that Nelson Eddy had when he was a member of the choir. The sexton had to turn on all the lights for me. The rector was very gracious and told me things about his choir members. Nelson Eddy had been with the choir when he lived in Philadelphia and was studying at Curtis Institute. I asked if he was a parishioner as well and the rector said, "Yes." And that Nelson Eddy had paid to have the stained glass windows lighted from the outside so the beautiful colors could be seen inside. He showed me the few pictures they had and said they had a choir robe that had belonged to Nelson Eddy, but they had no real proof of that.

About fifteen minutes had passed by and—I made my manners to him—and the rector said, "Is there anything else you would like?"

"Oh, yes, sir. Please let me get my son out of the car and you tell him all these things. He will never believe me." And I fled to the taxi, crossed palms with the driver and demanded that he wait. Pulling Chris into the sanctuary, we went through the whole bit again, not rushing.

Plus the rector said, "Mr. Eddy wasn't the only well-known member of our choir. Marion Anderson sang here for many years."

A double treat.

Dinner that night at the Four Seasons was elegant. And I have never slept on such a comfortable mattress in any hotel. Was I ever floating on air?

———•—•———

SINGERS—Two little girls about four years old were in the back seat of the car. We were on our way to dinner at a well-known restaurant.

They began singing, happy moments. Our guest displayed her talent by singing "Mary Had a Little Lamb," etc. When she stopped, my small daughter, not yet in school, belted out "Will You Remember," by Sigmund Romberg, all the way through, word for word, note for note!

Such a proud moment for me. I had not taught her this. She had picked it up from my humming and singing it around the house.

LOST COLONY—Sadness brings people together and we were in Wisconsin to attend the services for my sister's husband. After lengthy and proper services, religious and military, we gathered for the feasting that always accompanies funerals. And that is the same everywhere—more food than can be accommodated in one kitchen. My plate was finally filled, and I sat down to enjoy the company of her friends. Knowing very few of the guests, I made every effort to be on my best behavior. In an effort to keep the conversation going, one gentleman asked if I had read any good books lately. I mentioned a couple of titles. And then I elaborated on one book in particular, waxing eloquent about the Lost Colony. *Our* lost colony!

Eventually, I stopped to breathe, and said gentleman asked, "What is the Lost Colony?"

A very dull thud enveloped the room. My two children were there and reacted the same as their mother. Horror. "Oh that poor man. Please, God, don't let her kill him!"

I was immobilized. How could anyone anywhere not know about Sir Walter Raleigh's Lost Colony? So important to our history. I was shaking with fright and anger at the same time. I have always said that stupidity is unforgivable, but ignorance has to be accepted. A history lesson followed. Ginia and Chris felt so sorry for everybody.

The result was that the uninformed one agreed to bring his family to that very spot for their next vacation.

I still cannot believe it. I cannot remember not knowing about that bit of history and mystery and hoping that someone will solve the mystery before I die.

ANNAPOLIS—We were in Annapolis to attend a meeting and tour of historic Maryland houses—and staying at a hotel on the water. The day was spent touring around Maryland, not on the beaten path (beaten path meant a bee line from North Carolina to New York), and Chesapeake Bay.

I love Annapolis for its beautiful old houses, especially the Hammond-Harwood House and also the Naval Academy. If I am touring by foot around the town, and hear the drums and band on Friday afternoon, I am drawn like a magnet to the parade ground, and off I go!

Later that evening, we returned to our hotel. All day as we roamed through town, we became aware of wedding festivities going on around us. And sure enough, that evening, the reception was being held where we were staying. Somehow, as the evening wore on we were gradually included in the festivities. The occasion made us feel like we were in Scotland, bagpipes and kilts heavily mixed with all the attractive people, and so colorful.

Finally, late that night, we stood on the wharf with everyone else watching the bride and groom being "piped" away in a tiny skiff and sliding away into total darkness as if they were drifting in a dream. Such a special moment!

FESTIVITIES AT THE GOVERNOR'S MANSION—That highway 301 stringing through North Carolina included another small town with dear friends of ours. They started out as clients. A smart, attractive lady from Atlanta was married to a gentleman doctor from a small town. No expense was spared to make her happy in her surroundings. Once, when we were attending a ball in the nearby capital city, they served as babysitters for our young daughter. And, since we were going to the Governor's Mansion to be with the governor, they insisted that we drive their large new black Cadillac for proper arrival. They were in a state of shock that we declined, though we thanked them kindly. Arrival by Jaguar sedan that had just come over from England was, to us, the ultimate in style!

Such a grand affair it was. My social instincts were completely confirmed, however, while waiting for the governor and his lady to begin the grand march. I overheard him say, in an uncertain voice, "What do I do now?"

Another Governor's Mansion affair was at Christmas time, following a performance of *The Nutcracker*. Of course, I wore my new wrap to the ballet and the reception afterward at the mansion. The Christmas tree was gorgeous and the guests from all over the state were attractive and lovely.

We were at the end of the coat check line, waiting to get our wraps and coats so we could return home. There was one jacket left and, as the attendant helped me, I sensed something was amiss. It was not my coat! All the guests were already driving away. Someone, somewhere, was driving away with my coat–a new coat at that! The thought of theft at that elegant address barely crossed my mind. It could only have been exchanged by mistake. Horror! How many miles down the road to the coast or up the road to the mountains was my coat going to travel before it got back to me? The initials in the remaining coat, as well as the label, eventually solved the mystery, and joy of joys, it belonged to a lady right there in the capitol city. Coats were happily exchanged and our evening was not completely spoiled.

—•◦•—

The return of A. J. Davis to North Carolina in 1966 was something of a miracle! In 1966, this now prominent architect of the nineteenth century had disappeared from the pages of history as far as North Carolina was concerned.

Greensboro, one of the many centers of intelligentsia in the state, was having growing pains. Historic homes and sites were being destroyed in the name of progress—Urban Renewal supported this path of destruction.

Not only were we losing a charming raised cottage about a hundred years old in a lovely setting, but Blandwood, the home of a mid-nineteenth century governor, was endangered. The property had been greatly abused, but the suggestions by Urban Renewal, such as replacing the original tin roof, which did not need to be replaced at that time, would have been even more destructive.

Enter God. With an infant son still learning to sleep in the nighttime, Henry Zenke and I would take turns sleeping in the same room with him. It was my turn. I was already in bed, and wanting something to read, I looked in my usual hiding place—under the bed—and found booklets I had put off reading. Among them was a National Trust publication on Lyndhurst— a trust property in Tarrytown, New York. I was totally disinterested in that style of architecture, but I did decide to read the article on its architect, a man named A.J. Davis.

Halfway through the article, there was a paragraph that identified him with the North Carolina State House, his visits to North Carolina and his "advanced fenestration in his buildings!" "Excalibur!" Was it possible? Davis had been in North Carolina about the time of Governor Morehead's term of office. Was it possible that he had influenced the governor? Was it possible that this well-known (at that time) architect had designed the house that was about to be destroyed?

I knew this information was a large tool that could be used to influence people with more power than urban renewal. How interesting and how unbelievable!

A commission had been formed years ago to consider saving it because it was a governor's home. Somehow this commission stayed in existence even though its members did not like that style of architecture.

And what was the style? A five part, Tuscan Villa that had been wrapped around a simple 1790 farmhouse, and an early symmetrical form, perhaps a prototype.

An important, well-organized, service group appointed a fact-finding committee. The results of their study were that the large, five-part plan should be destroyed and the 1790 farmhouse saved!

Midnight. Who should I call about my deduction? The governor's great, great granddaughter, a friend of mine, would not appreciate a call at this time of night! What to do? I'll think about that tomorrow. No, I cannot. I might die in the middle of the night and no one would ever know. Horrible thought. Nothing to do but tell Henry Zenke tonight.

Now! Waking Henry from a deep sleep was a dangerous thing, but wake him I did.

Slowly, quietly, I said, "Hank. Hank, dear." (I used a term of endearment) "Please don't wake up, but I think I've found the architect of Blandwood."

Large groan. "You mean that place had an architect?"

"Please, Hank, listen to me carefully. It was a man from New York, his name was A.J. Davis, now go back to sleep!"

Morning came, 7:30 A.M.—coffee time. After perusing the newspaper (first things first), Henry finally spoke. "Now, what's this about Blandwood having an architect? Who was it, Frank Lloyd Wright (affectionately known as Frank Lloyd Wrong in our household)?"

"I really think I'm onto something, just give me a little time to check this out," I said.

My first call was to the North Carolina Department of Archives. Outlining my thoughts, I suggested that they flip through the governor's papers and see if there was any mention of Davis.

"Virginia, dear, you come down here and flip through them yourself. They have never been catalogued and they are all over the place."

Undaunted, I decided, on Friday night, to call a friend, Tempie Prince of High Rock Farm, a former officer of the then Antiquities Society who possessed a fine library of North Carolina history.

I outlined my thoughts to her, only to have her say, "Virginia, I know how interested you are in this, but it is the weekend and I have to pay the farm workers. And, besides that, the sheep shearers are coming, and I simply do not have time to bother with this."

Saturday morning, 7:30 A.M., the phone rings, the historian in Tempie surmounted everything else. "Virginia, I have found an article in the *North Carolina Historical Quarterly*, by John Allcott of the University at Chapel Hill, which states that while in the area, Davis visited Greensboro and later designed a villa for Governor John Motley Morehead."

Eureka! Excalibur for sure!

Then I informed the Governor's great great granddaughter, who was pleased. Then I informed Mrs. Kellenberger, a friend of ours of Tryon Palace fame. Of course, I thought she would say, "How wonderful, Virginia, I will be glad to underwrite your project." Wishful thinking on my part. The rest is history.

A newspaperwoman, Eleanor Dare Kennedy, responded to my plea. She was at the late, great Woman's College with me. She understood immediately the importance of this, that Blandwood was locally important as an old house, important to the state as a governor's home, and important nationally as one of the few remaining domiciles designed by A.J. Davis.

Weekly articles appeared in the local paper and Martha Long covered all events. A friend, a professor of history at UNCG, Walter Luczynski, went to the Metropolitan Museum in New York and located the drawings of Blandwood by Davis and brought copies back to me. They had previously been noted in John Allcott's article and one of A.J. Downing's books.

Newspapers (including the *New York Times*) and art magazines (including *Antiques*) made references to Davis and his importance.

At the annual meeting, the North Carolina Antiquities Society granted me two minutes to present my story. The people of Greensboro responded, and on a freezing cold winter Sunday afternoon, over six hundred people came up the hill to see this much damaged, but important, structure.

The ball was rolling. The Greensboro Preservation Society was founded (now Preservation Greensboro) with much help from Governor Morehead's family and the Morehead Commission. Other organizations came forth with help, also John Allcott and Buffie Ives, sister of Adlai Stevenson.

And Henry Zenke has never laughed at my guesswork since. He completely supported and led our efforts to save this important structure. John Allcott had identified Davis years before, but it took a history buff disguised as a decorator to establish his importance locally.

It was my big moment! With much help from many people, that bandwagon became loaded!

TAROVER—It was the spring of 1969—April—the last week of that month, and we had been invited to Camden, South Carolina to visit historic sites. The pleasure of meeting Bill Buckley's mother also held a lot of attraction for us.

With Blandwood well on the way to being restored, Henry and I began to sit up and take notice of other nineteenth century structures and let that curtain slowly rise to reveal interesting artifacts that we had never noticed—or been allowed to notice.

Just before we were to go to Camden, we were invited on a house tour and luncheon in Halifax, Virginia. Now if you want to behold a person in torment, it is Virginia Ford Zenke when she has to choose between the state of South Carolina and the state of Virginia. I suppose that is why I am so content living in North Carolina.

It had always been a hidden problem—one that would not go away: in which state would I want to possess the dream plantation house? The thought has occupied so much of my thinking time.

Feeling that the problem was only an academic one, I spent my time drawing Georgian houses of Virginia with South Carolina moss hanging—dripping from live oak trees in the background!

My grandparents' "raised cottage" in South Carolina had burned. The Georgia plantation of my great great grandparents had been sold (now a club and golf course), and the one I really wanted from the family was in South Carolina, near Marion, and had also been sold. For a while it had been used as a clubhouse with a golf course and even a little landing strip. The house was obviously influenced by Robert Mills, and now it was destroyed. My father's side of the family had a very old house—saddlebag style—that is still in the possession of a descendant, but much altered, on the land granted by George III.

The last weekend in April, 1969. I still had to work out how to be in South Carolina and Virginia at the same time.

"No way," said Henry. "This time, make up your mind!"

Curiosity made the decision. To and from college I had been through South Boston, Virginia, and I had only seen the miserable 1940 bus station. So, on Sunday morning, we packed up the two children and headed for Virginia. The town of Halifax was more interesting than I had thought, and seeing Redfields was the highlight of the houses on tour. Mary Lewis and Robert Edmunds were the owners who had restored his ancestral home–Redfields, and definitely influenced my decision that weekend.

We were standing on the front steps of Ashton Hall, then the home of Dr. and Mrs. Lawrence, when someone spoke up and said, "Have you Zenkes seen that funny looking house for sale up the road?" Thud! I recovered quickly and said, "What funny looking house up the road?" My antennas were working overtime. If someone else thought it was funny looking, then it might just be something truly remarkable. Look at what had happened to Blandwood!

"Where?" I asked.

"You can't miss it when you go around a bend in the road towards town."

The afternoon was drawing to a close. We had one more house to see and definitely had to get gas before driving back to Greensboro by suppertime. (Monday through Saturday, it's "dinner"—on Sunday, it's "supper.") Driving through the countryside, we both remarked how much the landscape looked like Scotland, where we had once enjoyed a glorious week with sunny weather and beautiful scenery—and even saw a monster in Loch Lomond instead of Loch Ness.

We rounded a bend in the road and there *it* was! The "funny looking house" was a perfect example of Tudor Gothic architecture in quarried stone. And it had to be a close relative of Staunton Hill, the house up on the Staunton River that belonged to David K.E. Bruce, our most distinguished diplomat. Henry and I both gasped! It was so different from the two story red brick structures of Virginia. We were both reeling off its possible ancestry and bubbling at the same time!

We came to the end of the bend in the road and pulled into the drive. Sure enough, there was a "For Sale" sign up, but the gates were locked.

"Well, that takes care of that, we can't get in," Henry conceded.

"Henry, that has never stopped us before. Get the hood of the car as close to the gate as you can and we can make it."

I was determined to get a closer look at this place.

All four of us climbed over the fence, by way of the hood, and walked up an avenue of old cedars. It seemed like a very long walk, definitely overgrown, weedy, neglected—spooky, even. I felt the Brontë girls must have lived there and kept their brother locked up on the third floor! (Have you ever seen the painting of them in the portrait gallery in London?)

It is possible to figure out the plan of a house from the locations of the windows, doors, and chimneys, but I still wanted to see the inside.

We returned to the car, but did not have a camera with us, and I felt very frustrated. Determined not to forget this place, I memorized the "For Sale" sign, the name of the agent, and the telephone number.

Arriving in town we stopped at a then Esso station for various reasons. Henry got gas, the children were made more comfortable and I went to find the attendant in charge.

"May I use your phone, sir?"

"Well, ma'am, I don't think so."

"Please, you must have a phone. Please, before I forget the number."

"Well, ma'am," and he took a good look at my Sunday-go-to-meeting clothes and said, "Ma'am, you don't want to use this phone. It's down in the grease pit where I'm trying to work on a car."

"Where is the grease pit?"

Not to be stopped at this point of my adventure, I went down into the grease pit, in high heels and all. I dialed the number I remembered and hoped somebody would answer.

"Hello?" a man's voice answered.

"Are you the man with that funny looking house for sale down the road?"

"Well, I do have a house for sale out in the country."

"The stone house—do you know what it is? It has got to be a house designed by John Evans Johnson, and it looks like a Bruce house!"

"I don't know who designed it, but once, it belonged to the Bruce family. Let me take you out to see it."

I was right. It was important.

"Oh no, I can't do that, but I would like to make arrangements to come back and photograph it."

"Let me show it to you. I can meet you there in thirty minutes."

"Oh no, I'm not interested in buying it. How much do you want for it?"

"Let me meet you out there in thirty minutes."

"Well, all right, if it's not too much trouble."

Back to the gassed-up car and Henry.

"Where have you been?" Henry asked.

"Oh, I went to the ladies room," I told him.

"That's not so. I sent Ginia in to look for you!"

"Well, I talked to the man."

"What man?"

"THE MAN WHO OWNS THAT FUNNY LOOKING HOUSE DOWN THE ROAD!"

Pause.

"Ginny. What did you do that for?"

"He will meet us out there in thirty minutes, just to look at it," I said.

"What are we going to do in this place for thirty minutes?"

Desperate, I looked down the road and said, "I guess we will get some hamburgers at Hardees." One had never entered my mouth before, but it did that evening.

We returned to the funny looking house and Bill Caldwell was waiting. The gate was unlocked, and we drove up in style. Oh, it was sad looking, all gray and dismal, but what an interesting place, even with steam pipes down the corner of all the rooms downstairs.

Bill offered to give us a key so we could come back. We said "Oh, no."

In noticeable silence, we drove back to Greensboro. The children were asleep and Henry and I did not speak. I was so busy decorating the entire house. You would have thought I was in church, listening to a sermon!

We arrived home and pulled up in front of our jewel of a house in Greensboro. Henry turned off the engine and I burst into tears.

"Now what's wrong, Ginny?"

"I hate to tell you, but I *like* that funny looking house up there!!!!"

He put his arm around me and said, "I know, I like it too."

By bedtime, we had completely reworked it, and I vowed to live forever with the steam pipes in the corners, and to live with its old curtains and dark colors if he would just buy it!!!! (The steam pipes went first.)

On Mother's Day, we put down "earnest money." On Father's Day, we made the down payment, vowing to relinquish all birthday, anniversary, and Christmas presents for eternity.

By this time, I had delivered mattresses, springs, and one lamp to be carried from room to room as needed. Closing date had arrived, attended by all those people who watch you borrow large amounts of money. Even a state senator was on hand to see this piece of property "move."

The tears came. I could not help it.

"Now what's wrong Ginny?" Henry asked.

Between sobs I revealed my age-old dilemma—"It's not in South Carolina!"

I am certain that if a transaction such as this had taken place in South Carolina, the tears would have been the same and I would have replied, "but it is not in Virginia."

I'm writing this as I sit on the terrace of that house, named Tarover, a

Scottish term—does it mean "to tower over?" and I'm gazing out through now much-loved gothic arches, no less, at green fields, clipped and manicured. The tin top roof is painted a beige color to warm up the stone and I am thinking of all the work and effort put into this place by Henry, Ginia, Chris, and me, all because I wanted to.

Over the hill, on the horizon, once snaked the oldest railroad in Virginia, on the banks alongside the Dan River. Jefferson Davis and his cabinet fled deeper into the south on that railroad. The river road in front

of the house has seen, who knows, traveling from the deep south of New Orleans to Philadelphia, and Washington—John C. Calhoun, Robert Mills? I can dream, can't I?

———•◦•———

HALIFAX—One Sunday afternoon at Tarover, I was enjoying my Sunday afternoon nap as the phone rang.

A dear and lovely lady called to say she had a visitor from England who was a relative, and would it be possible to bring her out for a visit?

"Yes, indeed," I replied.

Anything to break the monotony of a "Sunday afternoon in the country!" My creed: I hate Sunday afternoons in the country; I hate Sunday afternoons; period!

I quickly patted up the pillows and wrestled with the newspapers, and soon the visitors arrived.

The guest was presented to us and was dressed in a liberty print cotton dress, something cool and comfortable. Just like one of us. She did not, at all, look like she had just arrived from London's West End.

I often leave books open to pages with beautiful pictures of gardens and houses, and there she was, looking at the book.

"That's my house," she said.

The guest turned out to be none other than Nancy Lancaster, Lady Astor's niece, over visiting her relatives in the south side of Virginia. We were so flattered that her hostess would think to bring her out to see Tarover. And a most pleasant Sunday afternoon passed by. I guess I don't hate all Sunday afternoons in the country!

———•◦•———

The Atlantic was rough that spring of 1957. The Queen Mary rolled from side to side. Dancing in the evening was more fun to watch than to participate in. One lady's outfit consisted of a white dress made up of tiers of very deep silk fringe and, as the ship shifted, so did the fringe. This same effect was created in the bathtubs. Filling the tub with water, I was looking forward to the luxury of a hot bath. As I sat, the water from the faucet began to come out of said faucet sideways, first to the left, and then slowly to the right! Thoughts of bathing left my mind and I immediately got up and quickly dressed, preparing to go down with the ship. I will never forget those rolls of the Mary, and I think that was after the development of stabilizers.

We were about to land at our intended destination, Southampton. The dockhands were on strike and the ship had to be put into Cherbourg instead. This, I thought at the time, was a bonus and was certainly an experience.

Going ashore, we realized it was market day and I had never seen so many beautiful and colorful flowers. Hot chocolate in a blue and white tiled shop made me realize that we were really "down in Europe," Henry's expression of where he always wanted to be.

We had dinner table companions, who made things more interesting. Among them was a much-traveled couple from Birmingham, Alabama, the Kohns, and their friend Winnie and an English couple who were going home for a visit after living in Hollywood. He was a cartoonist from Disney Studios. Also on board was Victor Borge, along with his family, and Ron Randell, who played the part of Cole Porter in the movie version of *Kiss Me Kate*. We finally learned that a small Cunard liner would pick us up and would land at Plymouth—oh, I thought, just where my ancestors had begun their voyage to America.

We were informed that we must be up by 4:30 A.M., have our bags packed, and be prepared to transport our luggage ourselves. No porters.

At 5:00 A.M., we managed to get over the gangplank to the smaller ship. We were served coffee and what was supposed to be breakfast, and proceeded to wait, eventually arriving at Plymouth. Passengers were scattered everywhere, only the aged, infirm, and pregnant were given the use of staterooms. Class distinction, at that point, had been abandoned. Our group of fellow travelers and their companions consisted of very congenial folks.

We arrived at Plymouth at about two-thirty and by five o'clock, fatigue had set in and we started looking for the bar and were told it would not open—maritime regulations!

And oh, how I wished for that gift of Canadian Club that Henry said I would not need. ("Try to realize, Virginia, that you will be traveling in a more civilized part of the world.")

Class distinction returned. Landing was slow, very slow! A tender came out and picked up about thirty or forty people each trip. The mothers and the small children were to be pitied, but not honored. Trains were waiting to transport us to London. By that time, we wondered if we would ever get on the tender. We were finally served supper: a slice of cold ham, a slice of pineapple, and a piece of bread. Just as we sat down to the table, our numbers were called to transfer to the next tender and, as I walked away from that plate of food, I remember turning back to look at it as if I might never eat again. By eleven-thirty, we were on a train, on our way to London.

There were six of us in the compartment, five of us who had managed to stick together, plus a very aged and wrinkled redheaded lady, covered with lots of makeup. Everyone was sleepy, but the sight of her trying to roll up her hair in curlers in the dark, thinking that no one was watching, was just silly. The girls got a terrific case of the giggles and could not stop laughing—a strange expression of exhaustion. We were invited to walk up and down the aisle so the boys could get some sleep!

At one-thirty in the morning, we arrived in London Town, foggy London Town. Henry poured me and the luggage into a cab and off we went to the hotel. (Can you imagine the mechanics involved with rearranging hotel reservations, etc?) But here we were in the fog. Just like Clark Gable and Myrna Loy in the movie *Parnell*.

We checked into our hotel on Curzon Street, and guess what? It looked like a Hollywood set for Jean Harlow. All I wanted was a hot bath, so I indulged. It was becoming daylight, and I took a look out of the window to behold the absence of a building and the presence of an enormous bombed-out hole in the ground. I drifted off to sleep thinking only of war-torn England and the air raids. At 8:30 AM, there arrived a blast and I woke up, jumping ceiling high. So much noise could only be the Germans back to bomb again. Happily, the noise turned out to be a big brass band— welcoming us?? Henry picked up our Volkswagen and our tour began.

CAVENDISH HOTEL—My husband, World War II veteran that he was, seldom relived the war experience. He was very lonely much of the time. Assigned to the weather service, he was not in the line of fire, so to speak. Billeted with an English family in Gloucestershire, be became rather attached to them and we later visited them after the war.

The night shift was not pleasant, but neither was it unbearable. Arriving home in the early morning meant that his hostess brought him his breakfast in bed. A luxury he never got over and always enjoyed. He never stopped telling me how thoughtful she was!

Leaves of a few days or weekend passes found him in London where he met other families and enjoyed their company.

His favorite place to stay was the Hotel Cavendish on Jermyn Street. And this was Henry's big thrill—the proprietress of the Cavendish was none other than Rosa Lewis, of Edward the Seventh fame, known to television viewers in recent years as the *Duchess of Jermyn Street*. To Henry's delight, they would engage in conversations from time to time. The most memorable one was the evening he was going out on the town, and asked directions of Rosa. Rosa's memory was slim on the whereabouts of his destination. Rosa's commanding appearance and voice summoned an officer, of some rank in the armed forces of the United States—she could not remember his name, only his hometown of "Cincinnati"—and demanded that he help this nice soldier (enlisted man at that) find his way around London. Henry was so impressed at her cavalier way of mixing ranks that he never got over this occasion and his brush with such a famous figure of history.

Years later, we were in London, on Jermyn Street. Henry took me to the Cavendish Hotel, which was pretty run-down by that time. The only thing he recognized from the past was the Porters chair at the entrance.

<hr>

1980 WINDSOR CASTLE—Another pleasant experience while in England was the day we went to Windsor Castle. There was so much to see that we split up. The boys, father and son, saw one area, while mother and daughter visited Queen Mary's dollhouse. Now, dollhouses and miniature furniture have always fascinated me, starting with the very earliest one I saw and visited in the old museum in Charleston. Time and again I would study it on Sunday afternoons. Of course, the one at Windsor surpassed all that I had ever seen, and we had to tear ourselves away. At closing time, I was very impressed with the architect, Lutyens, creator of the dollhouse.

And later on that evening we went to visit the cousins of a Virginia friend of ours, a lord and lady, no less. And guess where they lived? In the very house that Edwin Lutyens had designed for Gertrude Jekyll, a miracle of design and experience!

———•◆•———

EASTER, 1957—"What am I doing here?" My favorite words when I get cornered. We were headed for our reserved hotel in Paris, traveling through the Loire Valley to Chateau country. No one had warned us that all of Paris would also be spending Easter weekend there. Stop after stop that Saturday resulted only in, "Sorry, we are full." Telephone calls elsewhere resulted in the same answer. I insisted that we try an inn in Blois, as recommended by Samuel Chamberlain in one of his books. We were welcome to have dinner, but there was no room at the inn. And it was so interesting—those half-steps all the way up, so you could not pause midway.

We had a stony silence of a dinner—I simply was stunned at the idea of not having a place to sleep. On my travels at home, I was almost always close to a relative or a friend who knew I was arriving. I really was so angry that I would not even speak to someone who wore a coat with the label of a boutique in our hometown! The lady innkeeper accepted Henry's pay and finally said we could have the use of her parlor for the night. It only contained a short sofa and two chairs pushed together!

I finally slept and woke to the sunshine of a clear and beautiful blue French sky. I do not remember much except that I went to brush my teeth at the nearest available source of running water, and that was outside. Touring the Chenonceau and Chambord castles that day was an experience. So many people, such beauty, and still no food.

At last food—finally some beer, cheese, and bread. To say that I was despondent was complimentary. I was sleepy, but still determined to see the Chartres Cathedral. Our uppermost thought was to get to Paris, where we had reservations for the week. If all of Paris was in the Loire Valley, I wanted to be where they were not. We stopped at Chartres as I had wanted to. One more cathedral was more than Henry could take. It was beautiful, if smoke filled, a moment to remember.

Dozing in the Volkswagen for a few minutes before we drove on, I was aware of a big black limousine that had pulled in next to us. Out stepped two well-groomed gentlemen and two beautifully dressed ladies in all their Easter finery—navy blue dresses, trimmed in white organdy and lace, straw hats with veils, and the ever-present corsage for Easter Sunday, just like home. I was so impressed! That is until I realized who it was! Friends of ours, Bibba and "H" May, and Walter and Margaret Brown of Burlington, North Carolina; and the big black limousine was really a small black Buick. I was already wilted, and now I sighed. If only I could evaporate! But they were so wonderful and seemed glad to see us even in our ragged state.

We drove on to Paris, rendezvoused with other friends and enjoyed the availability of the Ritz in Paris, thanks to Bibba and "H."

Moral of this story is—let us remember the bible stories. It was not the innkeeper's fault that there was no room at the inn. It was Joseph's fault because he did not make reservations for that historic night! For such irreligious thoughts, I became very ill. I had brushed my teeth with bad water and come down with some terrible affliction that lasted until we arrived in Switzerland.

———————

PARIS, 1957—We had left Paris finally, thankfully. I had been so ill with what is called Asian flu that I failed to recognize and appreciate the charms of that much-loved city.

We were headed for Switzerland, and stopped at Vittel on the way. We could hear the water bottles rattling as we approached. Henry was out of francs and had to go to the bank to get some cash. When he arrived, there were others in the same fix, and I know not why, but Henry and a priest had to climb over a wall to get to the bank!

Money acquired, we headed for the American cemetery at Epinal, near there. While in Paris, I noted that on almost every street corner, there were flower vendors, and I so wanted a pretty bunch for my hotel room. None were forthcoming, but as we drove through a beautiful and dense forest, there were people by the roadside selling, guess what? My favorite flower, lilies of the valley, in large quantities. At home, we could never gather more than a fistful at a time. Henry came to a sudden halt, and purchased a basketful of the lilies for me. It was a huge amount, stuffed in that little Volkswagen. They were so beautiful, and oh, the scent.

We arrived at the American cemetery and I could only gasp. Over five thousand Americans lay buried there, their graves visible as far as the eye could see! I was overwhelmed. We walked and walked and the scene was always the same. Tears came and my only thought was a terrible one. The next time Germany wants France, give it to them!

An attendant at the cemetery approached and asked if he could help us. We knew no one personally who was buried there, so I walked around putting bunches of flowers on the graves, choosing only those who were from New York, Virginia, South Carolina, and North Carolina. The only name I remember was a Holland from North Carolina. The attendant looked up his record and I think he was from Charlotte. I always wanted, and intended, to try to find his people to tell them about it, but never did. So I will just have to go to that place at the end of the "good intentions" road.

The remainder of most of my flowers was placed on an altar in a half-covered spot, and we offered our final francs to the attendant. He was not allowed to accept this money. Henry gathered me up, and with just a handful of flowers we got into the car, and crossed the mountains into Switzerland.

I was emotionally depleted by the visit to the cemetery, so I wrote a note to my father (World War I veteran), which he later took and read at a meeting of the Veterans of Foreign Wars (VFW), which added stars to my crown in Daddy's eyes.

My unpleasant mood continued until we settled into the lovely Hotel

Dolder Grande in Zurich. After a good nap, I woke to church bells ringing for evensong. There were so many churches throughout the city that I thought I had died and gone to heaven. It was such a treat to be there in that beautiful hotel. Services were so thoughtful. Even dainty footstools were placed under my feet at the dinner table to make me more comfortable.

—•◦•—

We were leaving Switzerland. I had loved our stay at the Hotel Dolder Grande, but we had to move on, and Henry was pressing for a decision: Did I want to see Rome, which was close, or Vienna, which was not as close? Why he had to ask me when he knew the answer was Vienna, I will never know. When we left home, there were no conversations, or even thoughts, of getting to Vienna. According to the map, we were at the point when we needed to make a decision. It was mid afternoon. The only hotel where we stopped was a very modern "motel" type of establishment, which did not appeal to us. So with excitement, we went on toward Austria.

It was almost May and the weather was nice. So, we headed up to the mountain pass, the quickest route to our destination. Our little Volkswagen tooled along at a steady pace. We were climbing, but very slowly. It was a very open but lonely road, no traffic, a very pristine part of the world. The houses looked like shacks—built very close together, as if they were trying to keep warm. When we got above the timberline, we realized just how high up we were. We had driven about thirty-five miles and started to ascend the peak to the tunnel indicated on the map.

We suddenly arrived at an impassable part of the road. Enormous mounds of snow and ice blocked the tunnel ahead. Henry stepped out of the car to look around and immediately returned. The snow was white, and so was Henry. He did not slam the door. He told me not to move or say anything. He quickly turned us around and headed down the mountain. When we were safely on the highway, he told me what a dangerous spot we had been in. An avalanche could easily have enveloped us. Thirty-five miles later, we arrived at the little modern motel I had so scorned earlier, and were grateful to find room and board.

A hot bath and room service was all that I wanted. I drew the bathtub full of water and stepped into an ice-cold pond!!!

The next year, we traveled to Charleston for an annual visit and walked into the Brewton Inn parlor. We related our experience at the tunnel to Austria and, by now, thought it was funny.

One of the foursome playing bridge said, "Oh, my dear, please don't laugh." And she continued, "A young couple I knew did that very same thing in Switzerland and they never returned. They were on their honeymoon and were enveloped in an avalanche."

A sobering moment and thought!

— · · —

1957—We had left Vienna, vowing to return again soon! Driving around Linz and leaving behind the Danube, we headed for Salzburg. It was a Sunday afternoon, about dusk, and there was a faint glow in the sky, which became less faint as we passed by.

The boy in Henry surfaced! "It's a fire! Let's go!" And off to a side road we went. The blaze was quite enormous in the middle of a field. To get near it, we had to just drive through growing grain, which was over a foot high. There was no road at that point. As we approached the flames, there were dozens of other cars, all Volkswagens, converging on the same point from every direction. We had to stop. Henry jumped out of the car and kept going. I elected to stay put. The source of the fire was a very large barn. Fear began to creep into my thoughts! Suppose something happened to Henry. What would I do? I locked the car and headed towards the blazing barn. I could not find him in the huge crowd. I looked and looked. Horror! It had turned dark, so I headed back to the car. Then it began to rain, and suddenly Virginia was all alone in a foreign country surrounded by the people who had been, a few years before, wartime enemies.

Panic really set in when I realized that our car was only one of dozens of Volkswagens, most of them the same gray, and I was lost. I eventually located the car, but there was no Henry and I had no keys. I had to stand there in the rain, not pouring, thank goodness, until, at long last, Henry arrived. I had envisioned him dead and buried by that time, and I really sobbed upon his arrival!

Somehow during this fright flight, I became homesick, and guess what for? Grits and red-eye gravy. Knowing that I would not find such a delicacy on this side of the world only enhanced my desire. The big hotel in Salzburg diminished considerably when I found that they had never heard of grits and red eye gravy!

The next day, we headed for Germany to find Henry's ancestors and, hopefully, some distant cousins. My only thought about each one was "What were you doing fifteen years ago?"

———•◦•———

1957—We had driven thousands of miles through the continent, and it was time for us to cross the channel and go back to England. We had found Henry's relations and enjoyed a nice visit with them, but now we had to be on our way. We had made reservations on the ferry from Hook von Holland and we were headed that way. We made a few stops along the way, so were headed for a late arrival. Henry had joined the Royal Automobile Association (RAA), which was supposed to provide us with any highway help we needed, and that it did. When we finally located the docks, the ship was puffing steam and blowing whistles. At 11:30, it was supposed to leave. It was now 11:30. Henry drove around some buildings and there, in uniform, stood the RAA officer. He sensed the problem. Our car was to ferry with us. He had us out of the car and up the gangplank. Before Henry and I got on board, our car had been lifted onto the ship, and we were moving away from the dock, a miracle of timing. And what an efficient organization the RAA proved to be.

We were ushered into mudroom-type sleeping quarters. I remarked, "But we paid for first class tickets."

"This is first class, ma'am. Otherwise, you would sleep in separate quarters, dormitory rooms for men and women."

We survived the night—my, how delicious that fried English breakfast was the next morning when we docked in Angleterre.

———•◦•———

1980—We were in Florence, Italy, our first visit there. We had planned to stay in a comfy establishment, which was very old, very small, very respected, and always full. In-house meals made it even more perfect, and having arrived that afternoon we were looking forward to a family-style dinner.

Henry was very tired, looking for the hotel, with horrible parking arrangements on Hades Street no less. With some libation and food, we began to return to a sense of excitement. I had no reason to think that I would run into any relations or anyone I knew there. However, out of the corner of my eye, there was a familiar face. Could it be? "No, don't be ridiculous, Virginia," I said to myself.

We had learned, along the way, that the president of the United States was to visit Venice, and that great preparations were being made for that event.

My thoughts kept going back to the familiar face—a lady dining alone. Could it be a girl I knew in college? She was of Italian background, or did all Italians look alike? She had gone into newspaper work with Time Life. What was she doing here alone? Time Life? Our president in Venice? As we rose from the table, I mumbled, "I think I know that girl sitting alone at that table."

Ginia replied, "Oh Mo-Thur!"

Chris also replied, "Oh Mo-Thur!"

Henry also joined in. "Oh, Virginia! Come off it."

Undaunted, as we passed her table, I stopped to speak. "Excuse me, are you from America?"

"Yes, I am," she responded.

"Are you from North Carolina?" I asked.

Again, "Yes, I am."

"I'm Virginia Ford from Woman's College. Are you by any chance Bonnie Angelo?"

"Virginia!"

"Bonnie!"

And we had a first class (or should I say, world class) reunion. She promised to visit with us in one of the parlors after dinner, and that she did. She was in Italy arranging the coverage of the president's visit for her publication. My whole family was fascinated by this editor, from Time Life, who had so much to tell about the forthcoming visit to Venice as well as the world situation. My stock rose to new heights that evening, as my family enjoyed the company of someone I knew from the past.

<hr>

1980—It was time to leave Venice. It was lovely and we enjoyed it, but we were all ready to get on with the trip to our real destination, Vienna! It was mid afternoon on a Saturday. The children were asleep in the back of the car and I was reading the map.

It was gorgeous, skirting the Adriatic with its deep blue water, pink sky, and the domes of Venice, all of which had a golden glow in the sunset. We were getting closer and closer to the turn-off to Austria. And then—staring up at me from the map was such a familiar place named—Trieste—just twenty or thirty miles away. How *could* I be so close and not go there? So much Hapsburg history was there.

"Oh look, Henry-we are only twenty-five miles from Trieste!"

Silence.

"Did you here what I said?"

"Yes," he answered, "but we need gas and I want to get into Austria before dark."

Silence—a fork in the highway getting closer.

"Why do you want to go to Trieste?" he asked. "There's nothing there to worry about."

Silence—oh yes there was!

Serious plotting on Virginia's part was necessary.

The Castle of Miramare was on the edge of Trieste, on this side. We could get a quick look at it and be back on the highway within forty-five minutes.

More thoughts! "Hank, dear. I think if I were you, I would think about this for a minute. Why, if I were you, I would not want to spend every Saturday afternoon for the rest of my life sitting on the porch at Tarover, listening to Virginia say, 'Just think, this time, a year ago, we were only twenty-five miles from Trieste!'"

"Just think, this time five years ago…" The turn-off to Austria went quietly by as we sped on towards—you guessed it—Trieste. It was in such a lovely corner of the sea. We got to Miramare, and there it was. The palace was not a very beautiful building—but the setting, the gardens, and the spell of the moment made up for it. The grounds and the gardens were lovely—hanging almost into the sea. It was all so gorgeous—but the thing that stopped my heartbeat was the sound of doves—cooing all around us—Maximillian's favorite "La Paloma" was all I could hear and feel. It was his last request to hear the song "La Paloma." How sad that he and Carlotta did not stay at this lovely spot instead of going to Mexico to be mentally and physically destroyed by the Emperor of France.

An hour and a half later—we all reluctantly left these beautiful moments behind us and headed for Austria. When Henry squeezed my hand as we were getting in the car—I knew all was well. Yes, we did find diesel—by the hardest. Earthquakes had just visited this highway, bordering Yugoslavia—and it was as dark and gloomy as any rugged mountain pass.

We all breathed such a sigh of relief as we drove into Worthersee—and found a nice pension for the night. Saturday fireworks impressed the children and they truly believed all the little dreams I had fed to them through the years. Austria was wonderful—after all—we were having glorious fireworks to welcome us to Austria!

The next morning, from under their eider-down quilts in little sleigh beds, the request came forth—"Daddy, can't you just hook us onto the back of the car and get to Vienna without disturbing the covers?" NO WAY, but a happy thought!

—◦•◦—

1980—It was Sunday afternoon—we had stopped for lunch–and we were hoping to get a little something to eat in one of those quaint villages off of the highway. Sunday dinner seems to be the same—all over the world—killing! We waited for an hour to be overfed with a heavy midday Sunday dinner. The local squire and his spouse were there holding court in their native costume. So very little attention was given to us strangers with the French license plate on the car.

We got back on the road to Vienna. Henry was very sleepy—he had done all the driving on those big highways containing jet-propelled vehicles. But reluctantly, he let me take the wheel. We were now in the country—south of Vienna.

They were all asleep—my family–and with no one to speak to, I could only wonder! What have I done? Will it be different this time—will Vienna have changed? Have I so over-glorified and romanticized that place that they will be disappointed? I was steadily driving in the right direction, but I knew I wanted to make a visitation to two places along the way—we were very close to Baden.

It *was* Sunday afternoon and there just had to be a concert in the square—I wondered if we could make it in time. I just knew we would arrive and there would be Noel Coward's Carl and Shari singing in the square (naturally, in the form of Nelson Eddy and Jeanette MacDonald a-la *Bittersweet*).

Alas, not so. But I went on to the next destination. I knew that by following the road along a river, we would get to Mayerling, and I had never been (having always been told I would be disappointed) so, disappointed I decided I would like to be. I was still driving and, this time, I would get there.

Henry refused to participate in this intimate little pilgrimage of mine and sat in the car with Chris. Ginia and I entered and, yes, I was disappointed, but there I was. Ginia again had an "Oh, Mo-thur" spiel when I asked too many knowing questions. (I have a copy of the "official" police report of that episode in history—I just cannot read German!)

Years later, Ginia and I returned to Mayerling on a cold snowy night in January. It was easy to recall the events of that setting, almost a hundred years before, and the horror of it all, as we drove over the same route from Mayerling to Heiligenkreuz, where Marie Vetsera was buried in secret.

———•—•———

VIENNA, 1980—A day to myself. I could not believe it. I must have walked five miles that day, not even stopping for lunch. I did not rush, but I did not lose time either. I was floating through the streets of Vienna.

Once I felt a little tired and slipped into the Scottish Church to rest. There was music, glorious voices singing familiar choral works—Bach, Mozart, Beethoven, Brahms—all very young voices singing in Latin and German.

It was obviously a rehearsal. The director was very strict and critical, yet they sounded so perfect to me. Their last piece was "Tenting Tonight"—in English. And I suddenly realized that they were young Americans. Sure enough, they were from Lake Forest, Illinois. I was so very proud of them. I finally got up the courage to go up to the altar to express my pride, and to tell them how good they were and not to let anybody tell them otherwise! The director was a little taken back that I was so forward. They all invited me to come back that evening for the concert. I could not. I had another commitment. I was going to waltz and waltz and waltz in a ballroom, just like in the movies.

The ball was being given in the ballroom of the Palais where we were staying. Now, it all seemed very dream-like—a very small number of young ladies from England, Spain, France, and the United States were being presented to Austrian society.

The guest list was straight out of my history books. I do enjoy meeting people and knowing their ancestry. Archdukes, dukes, princes, counts, and there was our own daughter in her ball gown, gliding down the steps to the garden and being greeted by all those young gentlemen. As she held out her hand, a handsome young escort took her hand, kissed it, and said, "Handshaking is for cowboys."

The presentation was ready to begin and, beautifully dressed and suited for the occasion, Henry and I went into the ballroom. The Corp de Ballet presented exquisite dances. The orchestra was wonderful, there were glorious flowers, and we had the most elegant cold supper, at ten in the evening, in the most beautiful small ballroom. It was even better than the movies. At last, the waltzing began in three different ballrooms, all adjoining, and we waltzed and we waltzed and we waltzed, just like in the movies. Pure Metro-Goldwyn-Mayer. It was tiring after a while, so I went up to my room and changed into a dress, that was easier to dance in, and fresh dancing slippers, and down I went to start all over again.

It was all very wonderful. Everyone was dancing, and the gentlemen, young and old, never let you stop! The beverage of the evening was orange juice or orange juice with champagne, no beer cans, no kegs of beer, no soft drink cans. Everything was very proper and lovely. Eventually, I gave out and gave up. Henry and I returned to our room, but not before I got a glimpse of our deb-daughter and her young brother wiggling downward like falling confetti and up again to the tune of "Rock Around The Clock." It went on for hours. I did not want the night to end. Eventually, I rallied to a very familiar tune, the "Beautiful Blue Danube," wafting through my room at three o'clock in the morning. We had just about "danced the whole night through" in the land of Johann Strauss, the waltz king, and Franz Joseph, The emperor of Austria.

———•◆•———

VIENNA, 1980—For twenty-three years we had waited to return to Vienna. Walking along the Ring Strasse always gives me pleasure. Ginia and I had been at the Kunsthistorisches, the great art museum in Vienna and we were hurrying back to the Palais. We had had no lunch and I needed to get to the hairdresser.

Suddenly, I saw a familiar figure about a half a block ahead of me. Why he seemed familiar when I could only see his back was a bit mystifying. Gaining on him, I still did not know him by name.

Ginia, I think I know that man."

"Oh, Mo-thur! You think you know everybody."

"Well, I've seen him somewhere before, I know," I insisted.

"Oh, Mo-thur!!"

A stoplight at the wide boulevard stopped him and his companion. I was there next to him. Should I speak? I wondered. I am still not recognizing this man who seems so familiar.

Finally–"Excuse me, sir—are you from America?"

"Ye-us, I a-um."

Instant recognition. Until that moment I did not know to whom I was speaking. "Are you Zubin Metah?"

"Ye-us, I a-um."

Ginia's jaw dropped. We introduced ourselves and had a nice little visit while crossing the boulevard.

"How did you know who I am?" he asked.

"Oh—we have watched you and your back so often on TV when you are directing the New York Philharmonic!"

And with that, he disappeared into the garden of the palais.

I very much enjoyed our encounter! And the next night he conducted Tristan and Isolde at the Vienna Opera House—five hours of watching his back and listening to a glorious performance of Wagner.

My fifteen-year-old son sat patiently through the entire performance, helped by his father, who told him the whole production was really like *Star Wars*. Ginia was spellbound and has never said "Oh, Mo-thur" since!

———•◆•———

ZUBIN METAH—One afternoon in Vienna we were invited to the American Ambassador's residence for cocktails. It was a lovely occasion, except for the fact that uniformed soldiers with machine guns guarded the grounds.

The ambassador left early that evening and when I asked where he was, I was told that he had left to have cocktails with Zubin Metah at another party.

Since that time, I have always referred to the occasion as "the evening that the American Ambassador had drinks with Zubin Metah and me (at separate locations of course)!"

———•◆•———

EUROPE, 1980—Traveling through Europe with the children was such a wonderful thing to be able to do. For them to see and learn, and for us to watch them see and learn! We had visited three of the hometowns of Henry's grandparents and were headed north to Bremen for the fourth. Actually, it was a little town called Outlader. So we went one Saturday afternoon in July. As we drove through the village (it was very small), we saw only a few unpromising houses, but there was a church, a Lutheran church. Appropriate enough. So we drove up, parked, and looked around, hoping that some of Henry's ancestors might be found in the records. Eventually the pastor of the church discovered us and politely allowed us to view the interior of the church.

By this time, we were a bit emotional about this visit and I sat down at the simple organ to play the only piece I had ever memorized: "Silent Night, Holy Night," and soon, the children and I were singing it, in German no less, as I had taught them. Imagine singing and playing that tune on a hot Fourth of July afternoon. It was something to remember. Conversation with the pastor was slow. He spoke some English and Henry spoke some German, so they got along. It did take some doing and it was some time before he wanted to know why we were interested in Henry's ancestry. You see, he was very suspicious of us and our curiosity.

Finally, he asked, "Are you Mormons?"

I fell apart and took over the conversation with an authoritative tone and explained, "How could anyone as Anglican as I be Mormon, etc., etc., etc.?"

The pastor changed his tone and his thinking, and invited us into his home, serving us ice cream and generally being very helpful.

It was time for us to be on our way and, as we stepped outside, a loaded station wagon drove up. The passengers spilled out and it was the pastor's wife and children, returning from the grocery store.

If you could have seen the look of horror on her face, her only thought must have been, oh no! Not all these strangers for dinner. I will never forget it for that is exactly what I would have thought if that had happened to me on a Saturday afternoon at dinnertime!

We returned to England, and were on our way home. We had given up the car and spent all of our money. We went for the bus to the airport, and guess what? We needed twenty dollars for our fare. Guess who saved the day? Chris. He had been carrying a pocket full of American dollars the whole trip.

———•◆•———

VIENNA, 1986—Hanging off of a mountainside in Austria is no fun.

My daughter had rented a car, and we were spending a Sunday touring the Danube country north of Vienna. Not wanting to miss anything, I knew we were near the Castle Artstetteen, where Franz Ferdinand and Sophie were buried. He was the last heir apparent who had been assassinated in Sarajevo, along with his wife, and, of course, WWI was the result.

We headed back toward Vienna, and I suggested we take the first road that appeared to take us up to the castle and the burial site of these two unfortunate people. As we inched along on what was less than a secondary road, the traveling became dangerous. Ice in this very narrow passage was almost impossible to cope with. So we elected to turn around. On one side of the road, the land shot straight up. On the other side, there was nothing. The road was only as wide as a car is long and we were going to turn around. Many minutes later, Ginia was still maneuvering and we were crosswise of the road, skidding every step of the way. Another few inches and we would be over the cliff. My last supreme gesture was to offer my fur coat in order to stabilize our wheels in any way possible. My admiration for my daughter's nerve and patience made me very proud of her. We eventually got into position to go back down the hill just as another automobile came inching and sliding down toward us. We safely arrived at the main highway and turned toward Vienna.

A few miles down the road, we came across a sign to the castle and the proper road to get us there. Undaunted, we proceeded up that road to arrive at our destination, all snowed in and not open to the public. Not even the chapel was open; but at least I got to see the spot where Franz Ferdinand and Sophie were buried. The rest of the day seemed uneventful in comparison.

———◆———

1986, VIENNA—Ginia was with a study group from Sweet Briar College— and I was a tag-along! It was about time for us to head to England. I finally got my courage up and asked Henry by phone if he thought it would be advisable for me to try to get to Budapest, or, if I should wait until we could go together someday?

"Good Lord, yes, go. I am so tired of beating around the Balkans with you! This may be your only chance!"

Then I really had to summon courage. The Russians were still in control and, chicken as I am, I regarded it as enemy territory. Surmounting all of my old feelings, except my desire to be a part of the history I love, Ginia and I acquired visas for a one day trip to Budapest.

We would go by bus through the colorful and quaint countryside. We left Vienna in the dark at 5:30 A.M., cheese sandwiches in our pocketbooks, so we would not have to take time to eat in a restaurant. We got on the "boose to Boodapest!" The driver kept up good speed until we reached the

Hungarian border and, from then on, he went forty-five miles per hour. I had wanted to go by bus so we could see the countryside. How lovely! Want to bet? Five crossroads and only one town! The weather in Vienna was all gray—snow and clouds—so we welcomed the sunshine and the ground being free of ice and snow, but the countryside was anything but colorful and quaint. It was gray, unkempt, and forlorn.

We arrived at the Budapest bus station at about ten-thirty A.M. We had eaten our lunch and were ready to tour. We had so much territory to cover before the bus left at 4:30 P.M. to return to Vienna. Getting off of the bus, I expected to be greeted and welcomed by an English-speaking guide and a driver with the car I had hired before leaving Vienna. But there was no one holding a sign with "Zenke" written on it. My heart was down in my shoes.

Finally, a woman appeared and passed as our guide. She did not say, "Welcome to Hungary." She did not say, "Welcome to Budapest."

She only said, "What for do you want an English-speaking guide with a "goot" Hungarian name like Tzenka?"

It was a fracturing thought to hear our family name, Zenke, pronounced correctly.

The Zenkes I knew, however, were pure German (not Hungarian) in thought, word, and deed. She elaborated by saying that there was a town on the lake named Zenke. Was my thinking correct in that the name had once been spelled Tzenka? Finally, she suggested that we go to the New York Café and have lunch. We explained that we had jut eaten and were not hungry. We were anxious to see historic sites.

"Well, what do you want to see?"

"Gödöllö," was my reply.

"Why do you want to see Gödöllö?"

Simple. I had read about it in history books and that was where I wanted to go! This was the Esterhazy palace that the Hungarians gave to Elizabeth and her family for their use while in Hungary. She loved it *and* the Hungarians!

"It is miles and miles away. We can't go there," she said.

"How many miles away?" Calculation put it about as far away as Winston-Salem is from Greensboro, maybe thirty miles. After more calculation on my part, I decided that we could spend one half of our five hours in Hungary by going to Gödöllö. A stalemate! And Ginia could see WW III looming on the horizon. Ginia was finally able to persuade the guide to "do as Mother wishes." The car I had hired was a beat-up taxi with a driver who did not speak English. He was large, but the car was embryonic. We got into the car and started moving.

"Maybe we should go by the New York Café to get you something to eat!"

"No, thank you. I spend time in New York City and do not need to eat at the New York Café in Hungary!"

Eventually we were on our way to Gödöllö.

We arrived at a small but beautiful palace—schloss painted in the ochre color, used so much in that part of the world. Our guide had to make inquiries and get permission for us to see the inside. Reluctantly, we were told we could see only two public rooms. This was now a home for elderly deprived ladies, and they regarded us as strangers. I was wearing my simplest gray flannel suit and cape. No jewelry, trying to look very plebeian. We did go in, looked around one large room upstairs, which had no furniture except for a porcelain stove that had smoked-up the walls, and one piece of furniture that had belonged to Kossuth. I could just imagine Andrassy and Elizabeth dwelling on Austro-Hungarian politics in this setting.

Time was passing and we needed to leave. As we tucked ourselves into the car, we noticed that our guide and one of the elderly ladies were having an intense conversation. We were then told that, since we were so interested in Hapsburg history, there was one room we should see if we wanted to, maybe. I said, "Of course," and asked where it was.

We went back upstairs and down a long hall, around a corner, and a sliding steel fire door was unlocked for us to enter the room ahead. It was a beautiful little "cabinet" room, very small, that seemed to be a library. And what seemed to be doors of steel slammed behind us, locked! Henry would never, ever, maybe, know what happened to us. Large photo albums and books were pulled down for us to peruse. The bus back to Vienna faded as I gazed upon family photos, unpublished, of the Hapsburgs, with whom I was so familiar. What a treasured few moments I had, locked up in the beautiful little room of French boiserie and brown marble, a perfect gem!

We returned to the car, reluctantly, to wend our way back to Budapest. I offered money for their kindness, but it was refused. They would have accepted chewing gum or cigarettes, but I traveled with neither.

On the way back to town, the driver only spoke to ask the guide what kind of car I drove in the United States. While I wanted to tell him about my nice and comfortable Lincoln Town car, I did not. I simply said I drove a Ford automobile.

We arrived back and drove around the city. We parked to walk around, and guess where we found ourselves?—right at the side of the New York Café! I was beaten. We went in and were served a miserable goulash and something chocolate with ersatz whipped cream. I did manage to get two small bottles of Tokay wine, so important from movie memories, as in Noel Coward's *Bittersweet*, with Jeanette MacDonald and Nelson Eddy.

We dismissed the driver and we were given a walking tour around the old town of Buda. We saw the cathedral where Franz Joseph and Elizabeth were crowned King and Queen of Hungary. We walked to the new Hilton and the shop where they had so much Herend porcelain stacked in such a quantity that I felt I was in some ten-cent store. It is no longer my favorite—it was too much at one time.

Back to the bus station and the same bus and driver were waiting to take us back to Austria. A long trip followed. At the border, we had to get off of the bus and give up our passports, and I got scared all over again. We were kept off the longest (good Hungarian name like Zenke?) of any passengers, but were eventually cleared. And oh how happy I was to walk into the Palais Schwarzenberg, my room decorated with Brunschwig & Fils wallpaper and fabric, a tray of smoked salmon sandwiches, waiting for me, to go with my quantities of straight scotch! Such decadence.

1986—A private little side adventure took place in Vienna. There was bitter cold weather here and there. Ginia and her Sweetbriar classmates had been invited out to "Grinsing" by one of the classmates and I was invited to go along. Everything was enveloped in snow, large quantities of it. We entered a large villa and the process of removing boots and heavy protective clothing took up the entire center hall space.

Once inside, I became aware of the fact that I was someplace very special. It was all Biedermeier—chock full of goodies, paintings, porcelains, small objects d'art, each one in a Vitrine enclosing all this. Eventually I was told that the original owners, and now descendants, had been jewelers to the Habsburg family, and most of the objects had been made by them. I was then looking at each item as closely as possible. And I almost thought I had found the missing Faberge chess set, platinum, but this one turned out to be silver.

On to the dining room—sweets, chocolates, and hot chocolate.

It was a memorable, memorable Sunday evening!

My only thought—How did they keep all of these treasures during World War II?

—————•◦•—————

ANNIVERSARY, 1986—In the summer of 1986, Henry and I were having a serious conversation and the question came up, "What would you like for your anniversary present this year?"

December was a long way off, so I did not think I needed to answer right away. But the conversation continued. "I don't know, Hank. You've given me so much. Something for here and here." (I indicated my neck and wrists.)

"Of course, I know. I would just like to have dinner in my favorite restaurant!"

"I just want it to be something special for you this year!" he said.

It was as if he knew we would not reach our fiftieth anniversary together.

No further conversation was needed.

December came and I had to make a trip to Atlanta. My son, Chris, was elected to drive me, and off we went on a Sunday afternoon, to return on Wednesday night. The next day, Thursday, as I was leaving the house, I noticed my little rocking horse that plays "Someday My Prince Will Come," had been moved out into the hall. Why? It had a long envelope tucked into the rocker. Oh, that can wait—I will put it back in place later. I figured that the envelope was just another paper Henry wanted me to sign.

I slammed the door. "No, that's dumb," I thought. "I'll just get it over with now." I went back inside, and tore open the envelope to read the card inside: "Reservations have been made for dinner on December 19, at the Zu Den Drei Husaren in Vienna. Is this acceptable? Hank."

Was it ever! I could not believe it. And off we went on the Thursday night before that date. After our arrival in Vienna, we went to the Palais Schwarzenberg, the opera that night, then dinner at Sachers. Then on our anniversary, December 19, we went to the Zu Den Drei Husaren for the same delicious food we had always gotten there. We had lunch the next day at Demel's. And each day was spent, walking, walking, in the snow, and then back home to North Carolina by Monday. Such a thrill!

I was glad to get back—and be able to eat at home, my really favorite restaurant.

———•—•———

SEPTEMBER 1997—It was a sad day. I awoke earlier than I planned in order to watch English Pageantry—the funeral services for Princess Diana at Westminster Abbey.

There was nothing unusual in my desire to do that. As a child I remember the then Prince of Wales becoming King Edward VIII. Shortly thereafter, I was permitted to stay up late to hear him abdicate. It was all very romantic, I thought. The coronation of George VI, his brother, got me out of bed early to listen to it (by radio again). All ensuing British events of state mesmerized me—coronations and weddings, and funerals—pure pomp.

So I felt obligated to arise by four in the morning, our time, to watch the unfolding of a very sad, untimely farewell service.

I fixed my English silver tray for coffee from a silver English jug—and two stems of roses in an Irish Waterford vase added to my pleasure. I then placed a linen nappy on my lap, and proceeded to drink my coffee from an English bone china coffee cup that was made in 1944 for an English "man of war." It rattled properly as I sat and sipped under framed memorabilia— two place cards, one for the then duke of Wellington, and one for Mrs. Virginia F. Zenke, as I sat to his right—for a beautiful luncheon on a sunny

Carolina Sunday at one of the oldest plantations in South Carolina. As the service unfolded, memories came back.

The prime minister read from scripture: "When I was a child, I spoke as a child…I put away childish things."

My first memory of going to school includes that first assembly—or chapel, as we were allowed to call it then—in first grade in a small school, and I can still hear the principal as he read from Corinthians—"When I was a child…"

I held together until the boy's choir sang to the tune of "Londonderry Air." Memories of my being encouraged to sing and audition for a radio program on WTAR, at age twelve, swelled up in me. As "Danny Boy," it was nothing to rave about at that time.

And then the Dean of Westminster spoke at the same spot where he administered communion to me when last we were in AngleTerre. I remember my walk back to the hotel from Westminster, passing St. James Palace and Chapel.

By the television, surrounded by English effects, I spent that day in England and recalled better memories of happenings at the Ritz in Paris.

POSTSCRIPT—I recall an evening—1957—when we were in Paris at the Ritz. After much socializing with friends from America, (George was the memorable bartender) we eventually gathered ourselves together and the eight of us went on to dinner elsewhere. We were traveling around Paris late at night. Traffic being what it is there, I should say, weaving around Paris. Frightful thoughts!!!

1980—A happier evening at the Ritz in Paris was the first trip with the children. Everyone had recommended that we have dinner on one of the Seine River boats, to go sightseeing. As we had driven up and down both banks several times, I had a better idea, which Henry thought was too expensive—the Ritz for dinner. Henry finally settled for drinks in the garden at the Ritz, and how very pleasant it was. There were so few people in the dining room. Reason prevailed and we went in to dinner. And a more elegant occasion I cannot remember. The melon we were served looked like a piece of Chelsea porcelain. It was all unbelievable, and, as we departed at the end of the evening, I stood and admired it all. The waiter gathered up an armful of the beautiful roses from the center of the room and put them all in my arms to take to our hotel. It was all very magical—a beautiful occasion for all of us, and the food was excellent.

1990—The evening in 1980 engrossed my mind for ten years, so the next visit to Paris drove me to make arrangements to relive that fun time! Reservations were made accordingly and after waiting endlessly for a taxi, we were forced to hire a limousine to get us to the Ritz. Upon arrival, and to my dismay, we were put in a crowded room that could only be called a grillroom. And there we were, all the flames and steam swirling around us. It was nothing like our previous visit. We finally were served—a small piece of filet for me, and guess what it included? A copper staple the size of a fingernail. Thankfully, I did not swallow it. Henry said that if I had been smart, I could have owned the Ritz by midnight. (Mr. Fayed then owned the hotel.) And this is the dumb part: we were staying at the Hotel de Crillon, a very elegant place. Why, why did we not remain there for dinner for another elegant memory? Never try to go back in time, thought, and actions!

———+•+———

GARDEN WEEK IN VIRGINIA—Oh how I hated Latin! And oh, how I loved Latin class. Our teacher was a dainty former debutante, and was charm, itself, and always upfront and center whenever we put on a play or produced our annual show, *Patches*. And one of her favorite subjects in Latin class was the movie star, Margaret Sullavan, a native of our hometown. They had been childhood chums—and so we learned a lot about the now well-known "Maggie" Sullavan. They had been neighbors, also, and stories about passing fruit baskets through the upstairs windows were seemingly very eventful occasions. The houses in that old section of town were very close together and did not have driveways, only alleys at the backs of the houses.

Time passed and I always took a personal interest in Margaret Sullavan's career, seeing her on the stage in New York and in wonderful, though occasional, movies.

One day, Henry and I were staring in the windows of Abercrombie & Fitch on Madison Avenue in New York, and whose reflection do you think I saw staring in the same window? That's right, Margaret Sullavan, in person.

I gasped! GASPED! Then I turned to Henry, and when I turned back, she was gone, at least a half a block away—such a loss. I only wanted her to know that her childhood friend had been my teacher.

And one day, years later, I read that she had died, somewhat questionably, and that her services would be in private. She was to be buried with her family somewhere in the Virginia countryside. I always wondered where—wondered and wondered.

I love to tour the Virginia plantations, especially in the springtime, during Virginia Garden Week. One year, I really needed a change, and I announced that I would like to take a few days off to do just that. It was best that I travel alone. Henry was not able to walk and stand for any period of time. With the help of the children, I was free to go off touring. Of course, I had the bag packed and already inside the gassed-up car before this plan came up. It was a cold April! Getting a late start, I stopped to get prepared food for supper and headed to my own Virginia plantation to spend the night, finally arriving after dark. Thankfully, our caretaker was lighting the way into that dark, lonely house. When, and if, I am alone, the first thing I do after opening the house is to stop by the bar.

The next morning was cloudy, but I finally got a lunch packed and started on my way. At three o'clock that afternoon, I arrived at Menokin, my destination. It was, as I suspected, just a shell of a structure—still standing, and made more appealing with lovely arrangements of spring flowers in extra large containers filling the empty windows and doorways. The grounds were "neatened up" and, except for unseasonably cool weather, I enjoyed myself.

As I signed in and bought my ticket, the receptionist expressed shock that I had driven so far just to visit Menokin. Why not? It was very historic, so it was like a magnet to me.

I took the time to visit nearby Mount Airy and soon decided that it was getting late. I would not get to my sleeping quarters until after dark.

On the way down the peninsula to the wonderful Tides Inn, I made a mental note of all the history markers (affectionately known as "I-ron Signs") and thought it would be interesting to go back home the same way. Normally, I go back home by way of Williamsburg, no matter how far out of the way it is.

I arrived later than I expected, and apparently, the innkeeper was about to send out a posse to find me.

After a wonderful dinner (soft shell crabs forever), I enjoyed a sound sleep. The next morning, I was late leaving that pleasant spot, but after breakfast I headed for home.

As I had promised myself, I stopped at many of the historical markers and enjoyed doing so—especially Christ Church!

One stop light in a small town caught me, and as I waited, I gazed upon, yes, one more historical marker—another church that sounded interesting, but it was noon already, and I did want to sleep at home that night. The light changed to green and I proceeded on my way.

A few miles down the road I started talking to myself: "Virginia, what is wrong with you? If you want to see that church, you should see it now. After all, there is no one in the car to tell you, "you can't". No one to tell you that you have seen enough churches. So why don't you turn around and do so?" And that I did.

I turned and headed back to the stoplight. At that point, I read the sign, and it said that the church was another three miles away. As I did not want to turn around again, I headed in the direction of the church, St. Mary's White Chapel, a truly colonial structure dating from the seventeenth century.

Somehow, as I drove, I felt so liberated, being free to make my own decisions. And oh, the countryside was so beautiful. Springtime in Virginia is something special, dogwoods in bloom—the whole area protected from interfering signs. It was a glorious feeling and a glorious moment.

The road dead-ended and there, to my right, was this precious house of worship, for early Virginians, in the center of a lovely churchyard of ancient graves, and more history.

The doors were locked but as I savored this moment, two people drove up to enter the church—an altar guild member and her husband perhaps.

I bravely asked if they would permit me to see the inside of the church.

Again, I was properly attired with a headpiece and little white gloves.

"Why, yes, of course."

And thereby hangs my tale: The interior was just as well cared for as the exterior, and I could only emote over the ambiance of it all.

"How in the world did you get the parishioners on the vestry to approve of these beautiful colors?" I asked.

"Oh, that was no problem. These are the original colors."

It was beautiful blue with white woodwork, the whole thing quite a gem.

All I could think of was the struggles I have with my own church to keep it beautiful. I enjoyed talking with them and asked if I might spend some time walking around the cemetery.

"Oh, of course. You will find some famous people buried out there."

"Oh yes, I know. The Balls, the Jessees, are so important, historically," I remarked.

Rubbing his chin, he said, "Yeah, but there is somebody out there that's very famous, a movie star or something."

Thud! Double thud!

"Sir, are you standing here in the house of God telling me that Margaret Sullavan is buried out there?" I asked.

"Yes, that's her name. I saw her on television not long ago and she was pretty good!"

"Pretty good? She was wonderful!" I said.

I could not believe my ears. For thirty years, I had been trying to locate her gravesite. I knew that she was buried with her family somewhere in Virginia, but I had never been able to identify the location. It was a private service and all my inquiries ended up nowhere. And here I was. With help, I located her family and there she was with a simple matching headstone like the others. It simply said, Margaret Sullavan, with birthdate, death date, and only that long dash in between which tells you nothing of her interesting life. After all, she had been Mrs. Henry Fonda, Mrs. Leland Hayward and, I am told, could have been Mrs. James Stewart.

Summary: What made me stop the car, turn around, and find something I had been looking for, for so long? What or who was guiding me that day?

Finally: I arrived at our farm by dark, and stopped there long enough to call home.

"You will never know how exciting today was! Truly, a miracle came to pass," I said.

"What, Mother, please tell us?"

"Oh no, you must wait until I get home to find out and I will tell you all about it!"

I hung up, jumped in the car and headed home. A few miles down the road, I had a sudden, horrible thought! Suppose something happened to me before I got home and they would never ever know about my being guided by an unknown hand. I arrived safely and they willingly and lovingly shared my glory moment.

Another one of my digest of dashes that I hope you have enjoyed.

Epilogue

Beyond acknowledgements, there is much gratitude to clients who have made much of this volume possible. People such as the husband of a very loyal customer who, when asked about what sort of budget he had in mind for their dream home, declared, "Virginia, please spend what you need to in order to get the job done. I do not plan to 'put a lid' on this project."...

and the gentleman client, through many previous projects, who decided to curb his wife's desires and my talents by sending me a very formal letter stating that he knew how "costly Virginia and Henry could be." He put a definite limit of $31,000 on the whole project, period! The total expenditures came in at $110,000, which was promptly paid. They continued to be loyal customers for years to come...

and the dear widow lady who wanted her apartment redecorated—and allowed me $150 for the project, which I proceeded to use for the do-over...

and the unknown husband of a client's daughter, who was an officer in the U.S. Navy, and I had never met him. Awed by the military and its rigidity (and besides, he was from up North), I dreaded the whole project. He walked in the door and minutes later I felt that I had known him all my life and as well as I had known his wife and her family...

and the morning's mail one Thanksgiving holiday that brought a letter, from such a dear and valued client, giving thanks to God that he woke up in a "Zenke House" everyday, worked in a "Zenke Office" almost every day, attended a "Zenke Church" (known to him as the First Gorgeous Church of America), and dined in a "Zenke Country Club" in the evenings...

and to the special folks who honored me by asking me to do over one of the most beautiful houses in town. And simultaneously, let me do over a "company house."...

and families who were not speaking to each other. The brothers whose wives did not get along, yet I decorated all of their homes...

and one family, divided, and yet collectively they and their descendants and friends provided me with the bulk of my work for many years...

and when I lost my loved one, Henry, the thoughtfulness of a "would-be client" made me realize the genuine concern of others. Simply a telephone call from the Fearrington Inn explaining that I was expected for a visit of several days at my convenience, to be covered by the friend—and the perfect substitute for: "Let me know if there is anything I can do."...

and to all those members of the Friday Afternoon Club who have so patiently listened to these events when presented as program's entertainment for our meetings over the past forty years...

and to my church—for letting me help to keep it beautiful!

For all these friends and more I give thanks and am grateful because—

"Friends always are!"